D0747022

CAR INTERIOR RESTORATION
—3RD EDITION

BY TERRY BOYCE

MODERN AUTOMOTIVE SERIES

TAB BOOKS Inc.

BLUE RIDGE SUMMIT, PA. 17214

Acknowledgments

Special thanks are due the following persons who contributed of their time and expertise to make this a better book:

Bill Sturm of Sturm Upholstery in Neenah, Wis., who contributed generously of his time in reviewing the original manuscript for this book and provided much of the material photographed in the book. Bob Lichty, Iola, Wis., for the drawings used in several chapters. The owners and managers of Antique Fabric and Trim, Cambridge, Minn.; Clark Upholstery, Hutchinson, Kans.; Stacey Shoffner, Wichita, Kans.; United Auto Trimmers, Bonduel, Wis.; Hibernia Auto Restorations, Hibernia, N.J.; The Joseys of Dunedin, Fla.; Hides, Inc., Hackettstown, N.J.; The Clausen Co., Fords, N.J.; Acme Headliners, Long Beach, Calif.; Jim Willems and other staff members of McPherson College, McPherson, Kans.; Ed Beaumont of California Mustang Parts; and Bill Cannon, publisher of *Skinned Knuckles*, and others who provided photos and information.

CAR INTERIOR RESTORATION
—3RD EDITION

SIXTH PRINTING

Printed in the United States of America

Library of Congress Cataloging in Publication Data

Boyce, Terry.
    Car interior restoration.

    Includes index.
    1. Automobiles—Restoration.   2. Automobiles—
Upholstery.   I. Title.
TL152.2.B69   1981   629.2′6   81-9175
ISBN 0-8306-2102-4 (pbk.)   AACR2

Cover photos (top left and bottom right) courtesy of Mark Wallach, Ltd. Automotive Interior Woodwork Restoration.

Contents

Introduction

The word "restoration" has a much more sophisticated meaning in the old car hobby today than it did even a few short years ago. When our hobby was young, most collector cars were built before World War One. They were simple, straight-forward machines, largely assembled by hand. They were relatively easy to work on and anyone with a slight mechanical talent could turn out a reasonable restoration by then-prevalent standards.

Hobby growth, both in numbers of enthusiasts and in values of cars, has brought new pressures to restoration, bringing it into sharper focus. The emphasis today is on authenticity. The more popular the car, the more information on authentic restoration is discovered and circulated, and the more value is placed on authenticity.

There are still many hobbyists who consider a restoration simply a quick paint job, new tires, and a coat of paint from the engine from whatever color spray is on sale at the local hardware store. This hobbyist either ignores the car's interior or re-does it in whatever material suits him. Many people enjoy such "restored" cars and we do not wish to debunk their personal pleasure. But serious enthusiasts call this sort of restoration "fixing it up" and speak derisively when using the term. More importantly, poor or non-authentic restoration work adds little or no value to a car.

As the concept of restoration changed, the interior of the collector car has taken on new importance. Early collectors "fixed up" old cars for parades and generally ignored the interior if it was at all serviceable. If work was needed, they usually had the wife stitch up some seat covers.

Today's enthusiast is much more likely to place importance on interior restoration. Perhaps genuine historical appreciation has overcome simple nostalgia; or perhaps the modern restorer has a greater awareness of the interior as part of the overall esthetics of his automobile.

For whatever reasons, interest in interior restoration among hobbyists has intensified in recent years. There are specialists conquering this last frontier, but they are few and usually much sought after—and their talents are expensive. Men have, in the past, seemed to consider automobile trimming as a mysterious procedure that only a woman could comprehend, since they operate the home sewing machine and "upholstery" is sewn. Auto trimming was once a respected and rewarding task and the time has come to put it back into its proper perspective. It is pleasant but challenging work, and the secrets often turn out to be no more complex than a clever piece of carburetor linkage.

Furthermore, the blossoming of hobby suppliers in the past five years, many of whom offer pre-sewn interior kits and other time and labor-saving items (such as molded carpet kits) to the home restorer through club and commercial hobby publications, has been truly amazing. The advent of the Sixties car as a hot collectible has accelerated growth in the reproduction and kit field with startling speed. Interior kits are not only time and even money-savers, they are a good opportunity for the novice with a desire to learn trimming to obtain valuable experience with minimal difficulty.

Although many restoration stories still state the owner "did all the restoration work himself except for the upholstery," more enthusiasts are tackling their cars' interior work than ever before. If for no other reason, they do it because the cost of professional interior work has shot up right along with everything else. Interior restoration is largely a matter of labor and time is not a cheap commodity these days.

We hope to untangle some of the mysteries of trimming in this book, and show you what you might be able to accomplish yourself in renewing your car's interior to showroom or better condition. Please don't think this is a how-to manual. Over the years numerous methods have been used to attach and assemble interior components and you must research your particular car before beginning restoration. We do hope to impart general procedures that hold true for most cars of a given era, giving you an idea of what to expect. Our club address appendix should put you onto sources of more exact information for your special project. Whatever part of the interior restoration you decide to attempt, we hope you enjoy it.

Terry Boyce

Chapter 1
Your Car's Interior

Maybe you already have your old car. But then, maybe you don't. Or perhaps you are still looking for the "right" model to trade your current project on. Whatever, consider a hypothetical enthusiast looking for a restoration project. Fun and a worthwhile investment are the motives. A convertible seems a wise choice. They are flashy, fun and sure to increase in value since they have gone the way of the dinosaurs as far as Detroit is concerned.

So our enthusiast starts looking. By chance he finds two 1947 convertibles of the same make. Sheet metal and mechanics are about equal. One convertible has been outside with the top down for four years. The interior is a disaster—moldy leaves, gaping splits in the leather upholstery, even a rusty spring peeking out in a place or two. The other convertible has a clean and still nicely-rolled and pleated interior turned out by the local custom shop 15 years ago and it has a nylon top that has kept the rain and leaves out. It is priced $800 higher but at least his wife will come near it and the thought of what might be breeding in those leaves even makes him a little green. So he buys it.

Six months later, our man has joined a chapter of a club for his car and has learned how much importance other members put on authenticity. Smitten by the restoration bug, he decides to postpone the new dining room set and put real leather back in the convertible. The first step is to pull out every last stitch of the custom interior. A visit to an area upholstery restoration shop brings another shock. The difference he would have saved buying the convertible full of moldy leaves would cover only about two-thirds the cost of professional restoration, even if he did the dash by himself. By gosh, he says, I'll just do it myself. Before he starts, (and should you be in a similar situation), a few things should be considered.

PATIENCE AND CONFIDENCE

Interior restoration is largely a proposition of patience and painstaking craftsmanship. If these are among your personal attributes, regardless of your profession or trade, you may make a successful trimmer. If they are not among your better points, well, thanks for buying the book and say "hello" to your area professional interior restoration shop's owner for us.

Patience is important for the home restorer because what he may lack in tools and equipment he can make up for with time. That is the major difference between the home restorer and the professional (Fig. 1-1). Both

Fig. 1-1. Seat assembly in 1941 Dodge pickup would be ideal beginner's project. Pressed cardboard inserts on doors would require ingenuity.

Fig. 1-2. Cars like mid-1950s Pontiac in photo were trimmed in heavy vinyl. Often, only cleaning and restitching are needed to renew these durable interiors (courtesy Pontiac Div., GM).

can turn out top quality work, but the man in business must use all the tools, tricks and craftsmanship he can muster to keep his time expenditure to an absolute minimum.

What the home restorer accomplishes in eight hours with effort, his handful of tools, and the determination to get it right, may be done easily in two hours at the well-equipped interior shop (Fig. 1-2).

Confidence is important in trimming, too. When you find out how much good leather costs per square foot (that's foot, not yard) you'll need lots of confidence to start cutting up a hide, for sure. Again, labor is the most expensive part of professional restoration. If you can do all or part of the work yourself, the savings will go a long way on other parts of the restoration and you'll have the invaluable satisfaction of having done it yourself.

Really, the best old car is the one with so little usage or so much fine care that it needs little or no restoration. A car with an excellent interior is an especially wise choice, and worth a bit of a premium if it isn't old or rare enough to have much value. Interior restoration is a very democratic process with all cars being created somewhat equal. It may cost you as much to restore the insides of Uncle Ned's 1950 sedan as it would to redo a 1939 convertible that is worth four times as much finished.

EXPENSE VS. VALUE

Consider, too, that certain body styles, notably sedans, are among the most expensive to restore but the least valuable when finished. Big limousines and seven-passenger sedans are attractive and relatively cheap, but before you don your Godfather fedora and cruise off, check the tab on replacing those yards of moth-eaten broadcloth.

Many cars are borderline cases. The leather is dried and cracked, but not really rent asunder. The mohair is dirty and flat but not torn. On pre-World War Two cars, even the ones with nice mohair, the dash and

Fig. 1-3. Plush classics like Rolls-Royce with extra-special needlepoint upholstery call for expert restoration (courtesy Hibernia Auto Restorations).

garnish woodgraining is likely to be faded and the plastic trim is probably all shrunken and cracked. In these cases complete restoration can be avoided. The appropriate chapters in this book will tell you what can be done.

Even as a perfectionist, be just a bit forgiving of your car's interior if it shows only slight wear. This is quite acceptable and judges and public alike have recently become remarkably tolerant of reasonable wear on original cars. Wear is an indicator of age. It makes the car look old and, unless it really detracts, gives your car the genuine charm of coming from another age.

If your car does need a new interior, though, there are possible pluses in having a professional do the work for you. He has things you don't—heavy-duty sewing machines and years of experience, for instance. His prices are fairly constant and the more your car is worth in restored condition, the better a bargain is restoration by a professional. A $1,500 interior in a $2,000 car is quite a different thing from a $2,000 interior in a $35,000 car (Fig. 1-3).

Chapter 2

Materials, Fasteners, Tools

Two types of fabric are used in most antique, classic and special-interest cars: flat fabrics and pile fabrics. Of course, there are leather and vinyl, but those aren't really fabrics—we'll catch them in a moment.

Flat fabrics are woven without a pile or nap. They are quite common in older closed cars and are still in use. Some types of flat fabrics are found in the cheapest cars. Others are used in the most expensive classics. Well-known flat fabrics include broadcloth, worsteds, houndstooth check and bedford cord.

THE MOHAIR STORY

Pile fabrics have a nap created from upright strands woven into a plain backing, usually of rubber or a synthetic substitute when made for automotive use. Mohair, which is made from goat hair, is probably the best known interior pile fabric. Velour, a short nap type of cloth resembling velvet is another popular pile fabric. Mohair was originally used in the manufacture of automobile *top* fabrics before World War One, but it was woven into a flat surface then, without a nap like mohair *upholstery* fabric.

Mohair pile material started to appear inside cars during the mid-1920s. They had a "long" pile and were known as "plush mohairs." The early mohairs weren't very popular. Then, as the decade came to a close two important developments emerged that kept mohair in the automotive vocabulary. The first was a successful method of securing the pile; upholstery manufacturers learned to fix the pile almost permanently by impregnating the backing cloth with rubber. The second advance was the introduction of mohair velvet.

Featuring a much shorter and more durable nap, mohair velvet was made by weaving the pile between two backs. As the woven material emerged from the loom, a sharp knife split it horizontally, producing two sheets of mohair velvet. During the 1930s mohair velvet was very popular. Its upright fibers protected the backing cloth, unlike the flat-woven fabric that was prone to wear since abrasion occured on the sides of the fibers. Mohair velvet was standard in many middle-bracket cars and was optional in most makes. It was disliked chiefly by young children, who found it rather scratchy when they sat on it while wearing shorts!

THIS END UP

Almost all upholstery fabrics have a "top" end. It is especially important that you learn to determine the direction in which mohair and other pile fabrics lean so that wear patterns may be correctly distributed and minimuzed. Most pile fabrics have the pile learning down when the fabric is held with the "top" edge up. To obtain uniform coloration and best wear qualities, the material should be installed with the "top" toward the upper edge of back rest cushions and toward the rear of lower cushions.

To find the "top" of a pile fabric, rub your hand gently against the pile. Moving toward the "bottom" of the material, your hand should slide along easily. Moving it "up" toward the original top will raise the pile, giving a bristling feel to the material. If the pile is so fine that you are still unsure, an old-time trimmer's trick may help you find "top." Toss a dime on the material while it is lying on a flat surface. Strike that surface a few times and watch as the coin moves toward the "bottom" of the pile material.

REMARKABLE LEATHER

Leather is made from the hide (skin) of an animal. Most often associated with cattle hides, automotive interior leathers may also be produced from goat or horse hides. Some cars were even upholstered in pigskin. Leather is a remarkable product in that it comes in just as many grades and thicknesses as it would if made completely by machine. It ranks with the most expensive materials you can use in your car's interior restoration, but it has the advantage of being exceptionally rugged and long-lived (Fig. 2-1).

Anyone who has ever discussed leather with even a shoe salesman can tell you there are two basic kinds of leather. The two you will hear about most often are *vat-dyed* and *color-sprayed* (or stained) leathers. Vat-dyed leather has the color both on the surface and into the fiber. It is dyed by immersion, but the color may vary in depth from side to side, although some color will be evidenced on both sides of the hide, of course.

Color-sprayed leathers are just that; the color is sprayed on with a stain solution or even a nitrocellouse paint formula. Sprayed or stained leather has the natural hide's coloration on the back, since the color is on the outer facing surface only and has not penetrated into the leather. But its nature, color-sprayed leather shows cracks much more readily than vat-dyed leather since the color contrasts with the natural leather visible in the pore openings of the hide.

Leather may be produced in many colors, including metallics. There is also hand-rubbed leather, which may be vat-dyed or color-sprayed for a base color with a darker tone worked into the natural cracks and lines of the hide for accent. Hand-rubbed leather is expensive but very attractive. It was originally found on many expensive open cars and even some DeLuxe Model A Ford convertible models.

Upholstery hides are run through a band-knife splitting machine which produces at least two and sometimes more layers. The top layer is the only sheet from the hide carrying the animal's original exterior surface grain characteristics. It is the "top grain" hide. Other layers may be finished to give an imitation of this grained surface by embossing a grain pattern into the surface or a different sort of design can be embossed. "Plating" might also be used. This is a process in which the hide is passed through a large press on a highly polished metal plate to give it a very smooth surface capable of producing a highly-glossed finished leather. Today most cars are upholstered in top-grain leathers, but older cars used other cuts of the hide as well.

If you have a question about the original "split" of the hide used in your car you might send a clipping of the original leather, along with a self-addressed, stamped envelope (SASE) to a leather supplier for his description of the grain type and the availability of a "match" for it.

BUYING LEATHER

Leather is sold by the square foot, but is usually offered in complete hides by retailers. Your supplier can help you convert the yardage you need to square feet in hides. Certain areas of a hide are more suitable for various interior applications (Fig. 2-2). Hides may range in area from 35 to 60 square feet, with the average hide containing about 50 square feet of usable leather.

The supplier may indicate the weight of his hides in stock, a measure used to determine the leather's thickness. Two ounce leather is good for tufting, door panels, dashboards and such; while five ounce leather is better for bench seats, rumble seat cushions and other stress areas. There will be an inherent amount of waste in each hide you purchase, since they do not come off the animal in perfect squares. Keep the remnants. They might prove handy for making door panel kick boots, hood scuff pads or even replacing a torn pleat or tuft. Remnants may also be used to back weakened sections of older leather upholstery when partial restoration efforts are made.

IMITATION LEATHER

Imitation leather has been around for almost as long as the real thing, it seems. Older open cars usually had imitation leather somewhere in their trimming; on door panels and top boots, for instance. This stuff was applied to a plain canvas backing and was very durable—often it outlasts

Fig. 2-1. Chrysler 300 used special vented leather panels in seats. Special order of replacement leather might be feasible if enough buyers grouped together.

the *real* leather on the seats, but then it wasn't used in high-wear areas. Also, imitation leather was less tempting to the various rodents that attack leather.

Like real leathers, imitations can be produced in many grades and weights. It can be of such high quality that even the trained eye is unsure. Examining the flesh or reverse side of the upholstery is a good way to determine if it is the real stuff or not. Cracks may also be a revelation, since they may show the fibrous make-up of real leather. Real leather is usually more prone to cracking, anyway.

Synthetic vinyl fabrics are the most commonly found imitation leathers in post-World War Two cars. But the vinyls don't really have the

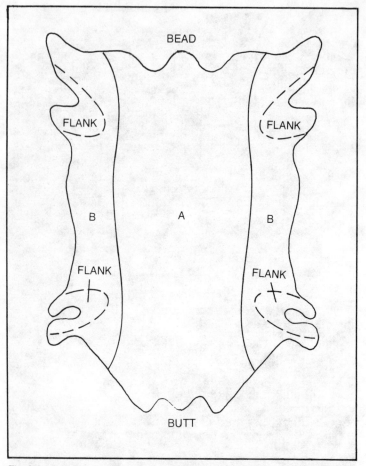

Fig. 2-2. How genuine hides are cut: Section A is the prime area of a hide. In this area the fibers are the heaviest and grow in all directions. Use Section A for seat tops, inside backs and other heavy wear areas. Section B fibers grow in all directions, but are lighter; this section is for lighter wear areas, such as quarter trim panels, etc. The flank area should be used where there is no wear or flexing as these fibers grow only in one direction.

feel of real leather, nor do they smell like real leather. The experienced judge's eye will probably detect the use of synthetics in place of real leather. If your car's interior was upholstered in real leather, it is probably well worth the cost and effort involved to replace it with genuine leather. It will be noticed by meet judges, other enthusiasts, prospective buyers and, most importantly, yourself.

Synthetic leather is sold under a variety of tradenames (of which Naughahyde is but one). It is usually offered in the standard 54-inch width, cut by your supplier to length.

OBTAINING THE MATERIAL

Finding the basic interior trimming yard goods for your car may be something of a problem, but not nearly so much so as it once was. There now are quite a few reliable firms catering to the old car hobbyist bent on restoring his own interior. All have a ready supply of at least a few commonly-found materials. Broadcloths, mohairs, velours and a really grand selection of leathers are now offered to the restorer through these outlets. Most advertise heavily in hobbyist publications (many are listed in the Appendix of this book, too). Flat fabrics and certain mohairs seem to be in constant danger of extinction as mills threaten to quit running the "low volume" orders from hobby suppliers (Fig. 2-3). The flat trim offerings change almost monthly, so if you can't find what you need right now, don't despair, it may be coming. Watch and read the ads carefully each month to keep track of the suppliers' stock. Let them know, too, what you are looking for. If the need is proven it will often develop enough market pressure to make a special run worthwhile. Most major hobby supply houses have samples of their products available. Some will send them free, while others may impose a small charge. If you own a car with a unique and very special weave you may be disappointed, but if you own a common, mass-produced automobile chances are good that someone can match the original upholstery fabrics.

FINDING RARE MATERIALS

Finding interior materials for an odd car requires the development of channels like those you have for finding rare parts. Locate and establish a

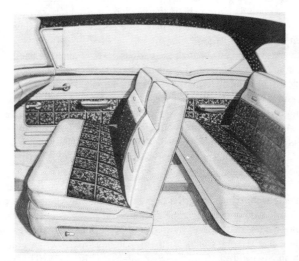

Fig. 2-3. Special upholstery weaves like the fabric used on inserts for 1959 Edsel interiors are almost impossible to find today.

Fig. 2-4. Rare authentic 1930s GM trunk cloth was found in rafters of trimmer's shop, went into prize-winning 1938 Cadillac 60-S.

friendship with your area's professional trimmer. Like many craftsmen, he may not be too gregarious at first and his time is his income, so do not bother him too much. He will have sources of wholesale supply that may be able to produce just what you need. These wholesale houses are pretty sticky about selling outside the trade as a rule, so you might offer the trimmer a commission to obtain the needed material for you. Of course, there is always the long shot he may have just what you need lying on a shelf in his shop.

Learn all you can about all the various sorts of material used in your interior before you start making the rounds of local shops. You never know what you might find on a shelf or in an attic, but you'll never notice it if you don't know what you are looking for. Example: an Oklahoma restorer, seeking broadcloth for his pre-war Cadillac visits an old upholstery shop. No broadcloth to be found here, but the restorer notices a roll of very hard to find old-time trunk upholstery cloth in the rafters overhead. Just one of the bits of "luck" that goes into a Classic Car Club of America "Grand Classic" winner (Fig. 2-4).

On later cars, especially those trimmed in vinyls, you should check with dealers merchandising the brand of automobile you are restoring. They may have some fabric lying up in the loft that was ordered for a job just like yours that never showed up. Sometime you may even find complete door panels. Don't pass them up if they are the wrong color. The vinyl can be painted to match your interior (Fig. 2-5). The new car dealership is also a good place to ask about convertible tops and windows. The larger the dealer, the more likely it is he will have ordered trim parts.

Sadly, the larger the dealer, the more likely he returned or tossed out obsolete pieces.

OTHER SOURCES

Careful scanning of the miscellaneous-for-sale columns in hobby periodicals such as *Old Cars Weekly* and *Skinned Knuckles* can be rewarding. An incredible batch of 1957 Chevrolet seat cloth was offered recently. Sometimes special deals on leather hides may be made in classified ads. A recent ad offered original 1960s Ford seat covers, found in a Detroit warehouse, to lucky buyers who acted quickly.

Your marque club may be a good place to obtain materials, too. Occasionally enough enthusiasts band together to get a run of an especially rare material made. The "waffle" pattern vinyl for 1955 Chevrolet Nomads and Corvettes is one example. You may also approach a manufacturer of embossed vinyls in strength by organizing potential customers from your club first. Most upholstery mills producing flat pile fabrics require minimum orders far exceeding the amount most clubs can pre-sell, however. For these types of fabric, it is best to work through an established hobby supplier.

Most reproduction fabrics are of very good quality but you should understand what you are buying. Sometimes the reproduction isn't entirely correct. A prominent Ford restorer showed the author a piece of Model A upholstery currently being reproduced. It matched the faded original cloth he held beside it. When he compared it to an unfaded piece of original fabric, it was evident that it was quite a different color.

Fig. 2-5. Expensive interior restoration might be avoided by obtaining good cushions and changing color to match your car's interior.

BINDINGS, FASTENERS, TACKS

Trim bindings, the covered cords that finish off trim, and windlace are readily available from the hobby's commercial suppliers. These businesses also offer a wide range of fasteners for your carpets and convertible tops. Fasteners were and are offered in a great many styles and it may take some doing to find the correct ones. However, most car makers bought their fasteners from the same wholesalers that today's suppliers do and a remarkable assortment of fasteners is yet to be found in these wholesale catalogs (Fig. 2-6).

Fig. 2-6. Fasteners used to attach rear curtain of 1916 Studebaker are typical of the era.

Fig. 2-7. Many of the fasteners on this sample board are still available. Others may be located at long-established trimmer's shops.

At least one major wholesale house, Auveco, sells to the restorer and is offering its catalog to the individual buyer. A considerable minimum order is required, which represents a large pile of fasteners, tacks and such. Perhaps your fellow club members can pool their needs with you to work up an order. These wholesale houses do have an incredible line of general trim fasteners for chrome strips and other exterior parts as well as interior fasteners. At least one hobby supplier, Nolan Tool & Chemical (see Appendix for address) is offering Auveco fasteners and supplies on a retail basis now. Your local trimmer might help you obtain these, too, but don't expect him to pass them on to you at his cost (Fig. 2-7).

Your local old-time trimmer might surprise you by pulling out a couple of boxes of the right top fasteners if you know what to ask for. Tacks, brads and tools of the trade are more readily available to him. Most tools and trimming materials are also used for furniture upholstering, a field that is much more attended to by retail firms.

If you have several cars to trim, or if you think you might like to pursue trimming as a part-time hobby-business you might start your own "source book" using a three-ring binder with photocopies of ads, source lists and the like inserted. The loose-leaf binder will allow you to keep your list up-to-date as various materials and products are offered and withdrawn.

THE ESSENTIAL TOOLS

Your basic upholstering tools, except for a commercial sewing machine, are simple to use and reasonably priced. You'll want a good tack hammer, with one magnetized end. This allows you to start the tack while holding the materials in place with your free hand. Once the tack is started, spin the hammer around and drive the tack or brad home with the striking surface. A quality pair of trimming shears, heavy enough to cut through leather or tightly-woven cloth is essential. Many upholsterers prefer 10-inch shears. You can obtain left and right-hand shears. Take good care of them, as they are an investment that will last for a long time if properly treated (Fig. 2-8).

For measuring material, obtain a square, a straight edge (a good yard stick will suffice) and a steel measuring tape. Tailor's chalk for marking on material is a must.

For removing old interior components you will need a tack remover. This tool, which resembles a screwdriver with the blade bent over and notched on the tip, is indispensable and will be useful for many chores other than that for which it was specifically designed. Some old time upholsterers used a wood chisel to remove tacks, but your investment in material mandates the extra insurance offered by the built-in leverage of the tack remover tool.

One of the simple tools you'll use with regularity is the trim regulator. Resembling a small ice pick, the trim regulator is used to distribute materials beneath the outer covering of assemblies, such as when working up cotton into pleats. the point will slip right through most cloth weaves. You may also used it to pop woven fabrics over brad heads on older cars that have boarded trim panels tacked through the material and trim board to wood. Keep the point of your trim regulator sharp and smooth; once you develop a feel for it you'll find just the right degree of sharpness you prefer.

You can begin upholstery work with as few as two needles, a long, straight, heavy-gauge sewing needle and a lighter gauge (4-inch or so) curved needle for blind stitching. Leather, imitation leathers, kapok-felted cotton, and other dense materials require so-called three-square-point needles that have a triangular cross section that allows them to cut through the fabrics for which they are designed, greatly reducing the force needed to push the needle through.

SEWING MACHINES

Unless you are making very minor repairs to original upholstery or are installing a pre-sewn kit, you will absolutely need a sewing machine at your disposal and you will need to know how to use it. Ideally, this will be a heavy-duty commercial unit. Your wife or mother's home sewing machine might do the job for you if your car is trimmed in light, flat fabrics. Don't count on it for tightly woven cloth and just forget it if you are using leather or an imitation leather material, because they need a walking-foot machine to feed the fabric and keep the stitching uniform.

You can manage with fabric that is suitably light by carefully feeding the material by hand through a home machine, keeping one hand on each side of the needle and keeping the pace just right so that you get good, evenly-spaced stitches. A strong, large needle should be installed for even the "light" trim material. Check the owner's manual to see if the machine is equipped with a gear reduction so you can gear it down for heavier upholstery cloth. The larger needles are readily available for heavier cloth, but make sure they will fit the sewing machine you are using.

A sewer who is very good can actually restitch old seat covers, top panels and such back together using most, if not all, of the original holes.

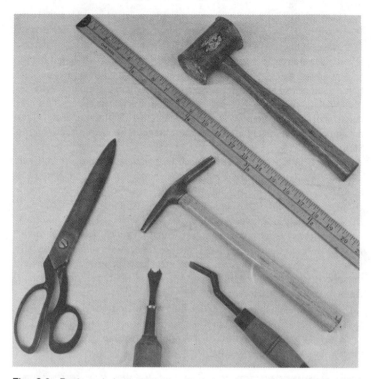

Fig. 2-8. Basic upholsterer's tools. Tack hammer, with narrow head, is magnetized on small tip. Shears, clip and tack removers, straight edge and mallet are frequently used.

This type of sewing is the mark of an extremely competent craftsman and isn't easily done.

Eventually you will conclude that if you are going to continue to do interior restoration you will need a commercial-type machine (Fig. 2-9). The frustrations of using your wife's machine, with its lack of power, inability to accommodate large needles and heavy thread, and the lack of a walking-foot attachment will just be too much.

At least two companies are now advertising commercial machines in hobby publications (see Appendix). They are rather expensive. Alternatives include seeking a second-hand machine. Look for these in the nearest big city where stores handling industrial cast-offs abound.

Don't forget to make sure the machine you select has the walking-foot. Some commercial machines used by dress makers are merely heavy-duty versions of home units and will not have the walking-foot. Buying a used machine—which may be as much as 50 years old— is as perilous as buying a used car, maybe more so, since you know something about used cars.

25

One of the best solutions to the sewing machine dilemma was suggested by *Skinned Knuckles*. They found that it is often possible to rent or lease a commercial sewing machine, just as many commercial firms do. If you can find a rental or leasing agency expect to pay $25 to $45 per month to rent such a machine, with a three to six month minimum time period. Some dealers will apply the fees paid to the purchase price of the machine if you decide to pursue a career in trimming. Furthermore, "usually the dealer will give you some valuable hints and tips about the operation and adjustment of the machine, so take advantage of his help," according to *Skinned Knuckles*.

Your first work will require much trial and error fitting, so you will need a sewing machine at your disposal for quite a bit of time. If you are absolutely sure the pieces will fit together correctly, you may find a commercial firm in your area that will sew the trim together for you with their heavy-duty machine. A good place to inquire is at your hometown awning shop. It is certainly equipped with heavy-duty sewing machines and probably has been in business for a long time, so personnel are usually very conscientious. Be sure that you emphasize politely that the work must be done very well and that you appreciate old-time craftsmanship. Remember, too, that if it doesn't fit, it is your problem.

The awning shop may be able to help on isolated jobs that are simply too much for your home machine, like sewing carpet bindings in place, for instance. The area's interior restoration shop owner might stitch the pieces, but expect to pay well for his time.

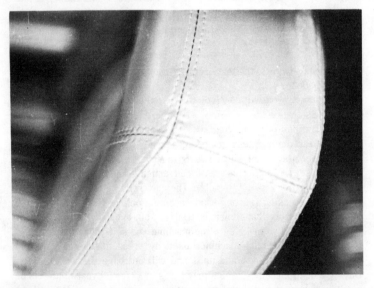

Fig. 2-9. Commercial sewing machine is needed to blind stitch vinyl, also for stitching through tough material on double stitches.

A PLACE TO WORK

Before beginning any phase of interior work, find a nice dry place to store the car and the parts which are removed from it. You can't wipe paint dust and grime off broadcloth with paste wax-cleaner. Most restoration experts agree that interior trimming should be one of the last projects in a restoration. You'll need a spacious work area to lay out patterns and cut fabric. A table or just a piece of plywood on sawhorses will suffice. Cover the plywood with something to protect the fabric from splinters. Plan the dimensions of the work surface around the 54-inch standard fabric width.

If you really get into trimming, you'll soon be adding new tools. Special tools are made for removing some makes' door handles, for instance. You *can* use a screwdriver, but a slip can rip a perfect original panel wide open. Find a supplier and buy the needed tool, if possible. "I still buy a new upholstery tool almost every day," one long-time interior restoration specialist says.

SOME TRIMMING DON'TS

Trimming automobiles did not change as much as did the assembly of many automobile components in the years prior to World War Two. Some básic rules were applicable to all cars in the pre-vinyl era. Here are a few, condensed from the 1930 Fisher Body Manual:

■ When pulling tacks, do not place the removing tool blade between the tack head and the fabric. You may slip and tear it. Always pry with the blade between the cloth and the board it is attached to.

■ Avoid striking the cloth with your hammer. Don't drive brads home with the narrow end of the hammer. It will mar the trim.

■ During dissassembly remember, restoring the foundation board panel can be a time and money consuming project if you damage it. Unless it is water damaged or already broken, keep it intact.

■ Learn the trick of slipping fabric over brad heads with the regulator. Don't let the regulator corrode, keep it polished.

■ While installing a pile material such as mohair, be careful, since the nap may slant and reflect under light. When installing a repair piece be sure the slant is running in the right direction so it won't show up as a contrasting part under light.

■ Keep the trim you might want to save clean while working inside the car; a wise precaution is covering it while working.

Chapter 3
Researching the Original

Now that you know a bit about the types of material that *might* have been used in your car when it was new, we will try to help you determine *exactly* what was used. Again, being authentic is very important in restoration (Fig. 3-1). Doing the job well is more than craftsmanship to many collectors. Your car should be restored with as close to the same colors, textures and appearances it had when new whenever possible. This sort of research can get amazingly complex. Ford, for instance, used no less than four different colors and woodgrains on their 1936 instrument panels!

Start your research with your own car. Even if it seems to be completely re-done inside, there may be hidden clues to what the interior was originally. Traces of woodgraining may be found on the lower edges of painted-over instrument panels or in the recess to accommodate the glove box door. Sometimes entire interiors were put on right *over* the original materials. Your factory door panels may be hiding under the vinyl tufts, and the original leather is often found beneath the same material on convertible seats (Fig. 3-2). (Don't expect to find good leather under those convertible seat covers, though.)

On closed cars, especially those obtained from elderly ladies, you might be pleasantly surprised when you remove the seat covers!

HIDDEN SURPRISE

It was quite fashionable from the late 1930s through the mid-1950s to buy a new car and immediately have the dealer install a set of those funny-looking twill seat covers with the red or green leatherette caps over the beautiful broadcloth, bedford cord or mohair. These same old ladies owned the couches you could never sit on when you were a child. They

Fig. 3-1. Unrestored cars, such as this Moon touring, rarely found as guides, are good sources of data if they are *truly* original.

appreciated fine upholstery to the point of not wanting to use it and did their best to protect it. By the way, reading hobby paper classifieds you will sometimes see low-mileage cars advertised as having "seats never sat on." This doesn't mean the original owner was afflicted with a problem requiring him to drive standing up. It means, simply, that seats have been covered since new and no human clothing has ever directly contacted the seat upholstery.

You may be happily dazzled by a perfect interior beneath the covers on your recently acquired sedan. Of course, you might be equally amazed, but not happily, to find large holes burned or chewed in the cloth, or big brown stains and other disturbances on that "mint original" upholstery the last owner claimed was hidden by twill covers.

The old-style seat covers are being reproduced, too, and they are a quick way to spruce up a tattered interior. Be a bit wary of "seats covered since new" unless you are in fact buying the car from the old lady yourself. Even then, be careful. Not all little old ladies are honest or have prefect memories.

WHAT IT WAS

If you are like most of us in the hobby, you will some day own a car without enough of its original upholstery to even whisper about originality. Or, you'll have one with such faded and soiled upholstery that it might as well be gone. Research will be required.

One great place for obtaining information is from a car you are sure is a perfect original. These cars are rare, especially among open-body styles.

Fig. 3-2. Although seats in this convertible were trimmed in real leather, door panels were imitation, as distinguishing age cracks reveal. Old leather has different appearance.

Hopefully their owners are the outgoing type, since they will already have been visited many times before you arrive in their driveway. In the event they are still amenable to your climbing in and around their prize, do be considerate and try not to damage or disturb the car. Carry a good camera and shoot for detail (black and white film may give better details since it is usually sharper). If the car is a convertible, remember to photograph the boot—in place if it doesn't try the owner's patience too greatly (and *if* he puts the top down—many show car owners don't). Photograph the trunk area, too. Don't forget to say "Thanks." When your own interior is part of a prize-winning restoration and someone shows up to put you through this, you'll understand (Fig. 3-3).

Ford restorers have an edge in research, but they need it. Show car competition among Fords is probably the toughest there is. All the Ford clubs have excellent publications and Model A clubs especially supply almost unbelievably complete interior restoration data. They publish many original factory interior photos.

At least one series of Ford books is in print, offering photo essays on virtually every Ford collector car to be found. These are restored cars for the most part, and the book's publishers do not guarantee 100% accuracy. These books are great guides, but your club is best for establishing acceptable authenticity (Fig. 3-4).

Join A Marque Club

Some other marque club publications come close to matching the Ford clubs, but not many. No other manufacturer has such detailed

Fig. 3-3. Original factory photos or low-mileage authentic cars are sources for accurate information. Cadillac factory shot illustrates special chrome binding on convertible top.

information on older models as does the Ford Motor Co. However, you won't ever regret joining a marque club. The club publication will at least offer reprints of original sales literature and ads, restoration stories and columns of parts and aids. Your club meets are great sources, too, and you may meet fellow club members in the same boat (Fig. 3-5). You will all be

Fig. 3-4. Original sales literature reveals wealth of interior information. Buick catalog for 1940 showed different leather colors and even broadcloth were optional on limited series phaetons.

able to band together for the reproduction of an important trim part that everyone needs (See Appendix for specific listings).

All major hobby publications can help find original sales and technical literature through their classified sections. When buying sales literature for interior research, look for the biggest (and most expensive—sorry) sales catalog the manufacturer offered for the year. The smaller brochures tend to emphasize exterior styling.

Large post-1920s sales catalogs are usually in color. They invariably feature large interior pictures and often have details of interior trim such as ashtrays, dome or side lamps and instrument panels. A sales catalog may tell you exactly what type of material was used in trimming your car but you have to sort out the information from the sales hype. Don't completely trust colors, however, since color reproduction was limited by the printing procedures of the times and is often "off."

The sales catalog will often show you what your trunk area looked like, too. Usually, a list of interior options is mentioned. This will tell you what options your car may have been equipped with. You can find out if leather was used just in the line's convertible models, or if it was offered on sedans, too. You may be surprised how many interior colors and top colors were offered. The 1940 Buick Limited phaetons, for example, could be ordered with tops in six different colors.

Maker Technical Literature

Technical literature is also a great aid in interior restoration. Even the shop manual and service bulletins, largely mechanical in content, often offer important interior service information, especially for problems that cropped up shortly after the cars were sold.

Service bulletins were usually issued periodically during the model year, then re-issued in bound form at a later date. They are relatively rare but usually quite cheap and they are sure to give you some otherwise never to be discovered insights into your car. Case in point: One popular early 1950's special had a bad habit of ripping convertible tops on the sides when the top was being retracted. The problem is hard to diagnose but a $4 set of service bulletins gives the treatment, saving the owner over $100 for a new top.

General Motors' Fisher Body Division issues its own service bulletins covering body sheet metal, upholstery and other interior trim (Figs. 3-6 and 3-7). It had been doing this for many years, but the older manuals are hard to find. Fortunately, reprints of the 1930 and 1938 manuals are available through hobby centers. For serious interior restoration, the Fisher books are hard to beat. The 1930 and 1938 reprints, along with various 1950s bulletins have been the single most valuable source in compiling this book.

Dealer Parts Books

The master parts book or parts list is a fine source of restoration information. These are factory issued books sent to dealers. Master books

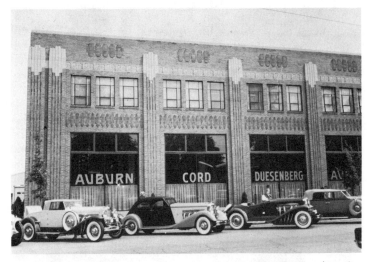

Fig. 3-5. Joining a club and attending a national marque meet is a good way to get restoration authenticity details. Row of Duesenbergs at Auburn-Cord-Duesenberg Club meet, at the old factory showroom in Auburn, Indiana.

list all parts available from the factory at time of publication. A 1956 book still has many mechanical parts for eight- to ten-year-old cars but will list soft trim for only two or three years back. Some companies have separate chassis and body books. The body book has body sheet metal and all interior components.

Other makers used an annual body parts list. These will give you fantastically complete interior information. Just one page of the 1937 Ford body parts list has the description of every part of the interior for each body style and what was painted, woodgrained, or trimmed in fabric. Often a book like this even says what *kind* of graining was used, the paint *color* applied, and what *sort* of fabric was used.

Before you can use parts books for reference you will have to learn what the factory called your car. The parts book won't call your car a "two-door DeLuxe Sweptline Stylesedan" as the sales catalog does. Instead it will be a Model 41-C, EA FB, 700 DeLuxe, 6219D, or something to that effect. Some place in the parts book a cross-reference chart states a Roadmaster phaeton is actually a Model 81-C and will be known as such in factory information.

WATCH THE OPTIONS

On early production cars, interior options were minimal. But on custom cars the reverse was true. You could have whatever your money and desire dictated. Most of us are dealing with typical cars, though. Model A Fords, for example, used many different fabrics and materials but

Fig. 3-6. Rare trim items, such as rear quarter ashtray on 1940 Buick Super convertible, may have been discarded by trimmers if car was re-upholstered before it became a collectible. Know what should be there before proceeding by checking authentic car.

almost every model had its own uniform interior. All 1931 sport coupes may have had the same upholstery but it was quite different from what was installed in the coach. Sometimes these set styles were changed mid-year, so you have to watch out.

Interior color and combination trim options started becoming popular in the late 1930s. To help service departments sort out the resulting confusion, most manufacturers started affixing a data plate to each car, usually on the cowl under the hood or on a door pillar. These plates have

Fig. 3-7. Carefully check original fasteners when removing old top—1912 Overland snaps are very faintly inscribed with Overland logo.

coded information on them telling what material, colors and options were installed in the body at the factory (Fig. 3-8).

A data plate can provide a wealth of information. The key to deciphering it is found in your shop manual or parts book (Fig. 3-9). There you will find exactly what your car was as it was assembled at the factory—its series, body style, color, trim, accessories and more may be listed. Understanding data plate codes also helps you to spot cars which are rebuilt wrecks, "upgraded" non-originals (such as a Chevy Impala Super Sport made from a standard Impala), and even stolen cars.

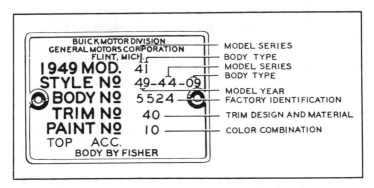

Fig. 3-8. Most cars built after 1936 have information plates like this one for a 1949 Buick. The trim number code can be deciphered by using an old factory parts book. Other important information is also listed on plate, usually found under hood on cowl.

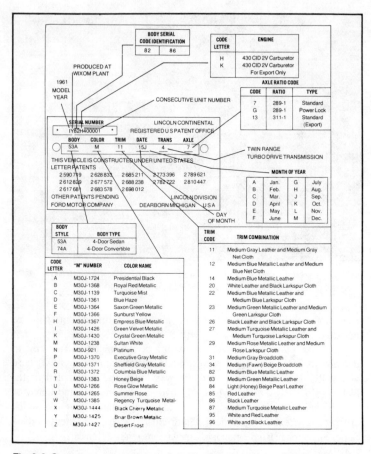

Fig. 3-9. Sometimes trim codes are listed in shop manuals, as this page from the 1961 Lincoln shop manual illustrates (courtesy Lincoln-Mercury Div., Ford Motor Co.).

Sometimes you are better off to ignore the plate, however. A Mustang with the fancy "Pony" interior is worth more whether it came that way originally or not, for instance. Some cars do not have trim information, which eases your conscience somewhat if, say, you want to upgrade your 1955 Chevy 210 2-door sedan into a rarer and more desirable Del Ray by installing the complete Del Ray interior kit during restoration. It is *your* car, after all. Maybe you hate chartreuse leather; how shocked you were to discover the dram car you're restoring was originally so equipped! You can put in any color leather you desire, but please be prepared. Some day a marque enthusiast with an elphantine memory and aggressive attitude is going to look at your data plate and inform you that it is all *wrong* to have beige leather in your car.

Chapter 4
Restoring Upholstery

Before the conquest of vinyl and other synthetic materials in the mid-1950s, most convertibles had genuine leather seat upholstery at least. Some cars, in both open and closed styles had their entire trim done in leather, one of nature's most durable materials. Many quality cars stuck with leather through the vinyl-era of the Sixties, especially European cars such as Rolls Royce and Mercedes Benz (Fig. 4-1). The increasing popularity of such cars in the U.S. brought leather back as a popular interior option during the 1970s, even though the convertible body style was passing from the scene. Leather interiors were rarely-ordered, but available, options for many American sedans before World War Two. Even Buick Specials and Lincoln Zephyrs are sometimes found with remnants of original leather sedan interiors.

Properly cared for, leather is a very durable interior material, especially if it is of fine quality. Sadly, before most automobiles reached sufficient age to be collectable, they went through a period when they were so valueless that no one spent any time or energy on maintenance of the interior. Leather interiors have usually been neglected before an enthusiast obtains the car.

THE ATTACKERS

Leather, or *any* upholstery material for that matter, is susceptible to four major classifications of deterioration. Variables in the environment, such as temperature, dust and grit, relative humidity and chemical compounds deposited on the material through air circulation may all have an adverse effect on the surfaces and eventually destroy the fabric. Rodents, moths and insects may attack the car's interior if it isn't properly protected. Bacteria and fungi may grow on leather surfaces, permanently damaging them if storage conditions are improper.

Finally, no matter how well you protect your car, if you drive it there will be the unavoidable abrasion of your clothes and the natural stresses of your body movements on the surface. To successfully protect a new, or even more importantly an aged but intact original interior, the enthusiast must know how to minimize the effects of the elements attacking his car's interior. Otherwise cracks from heat will soon appear and they will develop into splits if dirt is allowed to accumulate in them, working into the hide and generating a cutting action when the leather is flexed.

Unless you have completely written off any hopes of salvaging any part of your car's original leather or vinyl, avoid any sort of adhesive tapes as temporary repairs for loose panels and such. These tapes will remove the leather's surface when removal is attempted and may make vinyl permanently sticky. So *don't patch* unless it is a temporary patch for a write-off interior.

Convertibles are especially prone to have faded and dried-out interiors since they are exposed to so much sunlight. Stitches rot out and come loose, allowing the leather to shrink away from seams, leaving gaping openings on corners with stuffing and yellowing foam pushing out. Although nothing is more pleasing than a fully-restored leather interior, it is also true nothing is quite so discouraging as a completely rotted leather interior and a shredded convertible top flapping in the wind.

RESTORING LEATHER INTERIORS

Leather has become a luxury in recent years, far more so than it once was. (It was always more expensive than flat fabrics, though, for mass production.) Car makers pretty well abandoned it on regular production cars, including convertibles, around 1956. Special jobs still have leather right up to the present.

At the time of writing, quality leather is going for $7.00 per square foot and *up*. You can see why they don't figure in yards—too discouraging, for one thing!

GETTING IT TOGETHER

Old leather may be restitched if it hasn't become too dry and brittle. Working it up for maximum suppleness and flexibility will help it stretch back toward the split seam. Specially waxed threads may be used—check with a leather craftsman in your area for this—and if you are patient, the original stitch holes may be rethreaded if they are not torn out or weakened. Leather that is too dried out, however, may not stand up to the sawing motion of the thread and it will cut through the seam. Leather that is old and possibly too weak may hold if you can stitch in new holes near the old stitch line. Weak pleats and other areas, or surfaces with tears, may be backed by pieces of new leather glued to the flesh surface of the old leather.

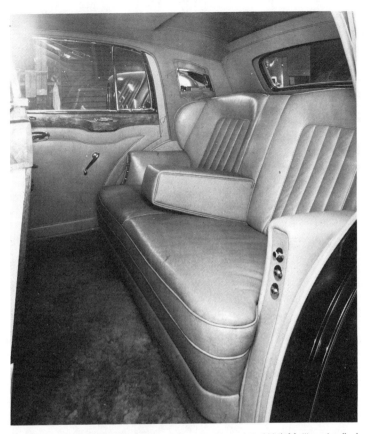

Fig. 4-1. Hand-buffed leather graces rear compartment of H.J. Mulliner-bodied Rolls Royce.

Many convertibles and hardtops in the Fifties had two-tone leather interiors, using white as the base color. These white leathers are often discolored by seemingly permanent black stains near the seat braces on the sides. These are often caused by a chemical reaction of moisture and iron on the leather. The black discoloration leads to rot, too. If your leather will come close to plated or painted metal parts along the edges of the seat, you can inhibit the destructive reactions that may result by coating the metal parts with a clear finish that will seal the metal. Black stains may be removed from dyed leathers by a very competent leather craftsman in some cases, using a specially formulated cleanser.

Restorers faced with marginal leather interiors were given a boost by a New Jersey firm, The Clausen Co., when they introduced their line of leather restoration products unlike anything previously produced. Their Leatherique process might just revive that marginal interior (Fig. 4-2).

Fig. 4-2. Full-leather interiors were found in most convertibles for many years. Sometimes leather is intact enough to be renewed with leather rejuvenation kit available to collectors.

No leather treatment can perform miracles, of course, but Leatherique can do wonders with a tatty interior that looks shoddy but is still reasonably intact. With Leatherique you can also successfully change colors on your leather and vinyl. The Leatherique finish seems to have a great grip on the leather and does not come off all over your wife's new outfit.

Changing colors is a possible key to a very reasonable interior restoration. In one case, the owner of a 1960s Lincoln Continental four-door convertible needing a new interior accomplished the restoration for under $100. His local upholsterer had quoted a price over $1,000. He toured area salvage yards until he found a decent set of seats for $35. Lugging them home, he ordered a Leatherique kit to change their colors to match his car. He now has an exactly-matched, very sharp, original leather interior in his Lincoln—at one tenth the cost of re-upholstering. You saw the results back in Fig. 2-5.

USING LEATHERIQUE

Leatherique is important enough to review a typical application. First, determine what is leather and what isn't on your car. Leatherique color finish will work on imitation leather but you might eliminate some steps. Or, you might prefer to use one of the new polymer synthetic treatments such as Armorall or a similar product on the imitation leather. Usually, you can tell the difference at a glance since the real leather will be more cracked and rougher looking than imitation material. Many early convertibles came from the factory with imitation leather on the door and quarter panels. By the mid-1950s, leather and vinyl were often used together in making up seat coverings.

Begin leather rejuvenation with a good cleaning. Clean the leather with a good wax and grease remover. Next, have the restitching and other repairs done. Your upholsterer appreciates cleanliness, so do the washing first. He will restitch the leather seams and edges. If he has to remove the covering to do this, sit down before he hands over the bill, but it will be worth it to get the job done right. If you want to try restitching yourself, special needles are available for hand-sewing leather. They are curved, allowing blind sewing, and they have a triangular cross section so they will not cut into the leather as they pass through it (Fig. 4-3).

After everything is sewn together again, you can begin the Leatherique process. To facilitate the process, remove door handles, escutcheons, garnish moldings and other trim items that might get in the way. It's like removing chrome when you're painting the exterior to make the job easier (and better) in the long run.

Even though you've cleaned the leather beforehand with wax and grease remover, clean it again with Leatherique's solvent cleaner. Clausen recommends sanding the leather with 180 grit sandpaper during this application. This removes the hard "crust" on the leather and cuts off grime patches, too. Wipe the residue off with a cleaner-solvent soaked cloth as you proceed.

Next comes the rejuvenator oil. This is applied with a brush. It brings the leather back to life, increasing its suppleness and giving it fresh

Fig. 4-3. Restoration shop repaired damaged tufts on this early touring car with new leather, then refinished old leather, blending in perfectly.

strength. Be sure to saturate the leather; rejuvenate it twice if the leather is extremely dry. Keep the rejuvenator oil stirred up or it will separate. It should be warmed a bit if the room temperature is below 70 degrees. Be sure to do a thorough job since the oil will be sealed in by the exterior color coating. After the oil has dried on the surface, you may sand the finish with 360 grit wet-or-dry paper, wiping clean with a water-soaked cloth. The oil rinses out of your brush with tap water. Save the brush. You'll need it for the final Leatherique coating.

Those small flex cracks in your leather are called character cracks by many. They say leather improves in appearance with age, that it takes on individuality, and so it does. These character cracks are enhanced by the Leatherique process though the rejuvenator oil may expose the natural leather color in them if your leather is surface-colored only. Don't worry. The Leatherique color coating will cover the natural leather, too.

Leatherique kits come with crack filler, too. This is for those larger splits and cracks that do *not* lend character. It is used to best advantage if applied after the rejuvenator oil. Use the crack filler only on sections that are solidly backed by a panel or substance. It isn't practical for areas like cushions where there is a lot of flexing.

Use a narrow-bladed, somewhat flexible knife to build up several layers of the crack filler during application. Allow 15-20 minutes between applications. Keep leather surfaces around the area being repaired free of the filler. After the patch has dried for several hours, sand the filled area with #320 paper being very careful not to scratch the adjoining leather.

The finish coat is the real Leatherique. Causen offers it in a variety of standard colors, matched to Rolls-Royce and Bentley colors. Or, for a reasonable fee, they will custom match your order. Send a clipped piece of leather from under a seat or somewhere that won't show and isn't discolored by fading. They are quite proud of their exact color matches, so don't worry. They will file the correct formula for mixing your color so fellow club members can quickly obtain the same colors if they so desire.

Leatherique is usually applied with a fine-hair brush. A brush comes with the kit but you may need smaller brushes to cope with piping and other areas. Obtain good quality brushes from an art store. Quality brushes are best since they won't trail hair all over the work. Keep the bristles fine to avoid brush marks. Leatherique can be sprayed on with a spray unit but the company recommends brushing. Since it is designed for brushing, Leatherique is not available in metallics.

The Leatherique color coating, according to users, works best in a fairly cool, dry setting. Sixty degrees is suggested by one source. Be sure you get it down into crevices, under trim buttons and around bindings thoroughly. If you don't work it into these areas, the original color will show when the seat is flexed. Try to avoid going back over slightly dried areas as they are more likely to develop brush marks. Keep surfaces from touching, like the bottom of the backrest and the rear of the cushion may do.

Clausen says to let the first coat dry for 20 minutes or so and then repeat the whole color coat operation. In about 24 hours the surface will have "cured" and be ready for service.

One of Leatherique's best features is its color fastness. Once applied, it is there to stay. Users report the color holds under all sorts of weather conditions. Another thing Leatherique users like is the way it re-creates the original leathery sheen of their upholstery without being too garish or dull.

Leatherique comes in three sizes of kits. The officers of the company are devoted hobbyists, too, and have lectured at many club seminars on interior restoration.

VINYL AND RUBBER

Renewing vinyl surfaces and rubber trim and sealing parts may be accomplished with one of several new treatments for these materials. Unlike Leatherique, they do not change color, or put a new finish on pieces. But they do penetrate into the material, greatly increasing durability and giving a new, live look. Tired vinyl is especially receptive to being treated with these products. A typical application is made to a thoroughly cleaned area by wiping the liquid on with a cloth. After a couple of hours the process is repeated. No residue is left by these products, but a buffing with a clean cloth does increase the sheen of treated parts. These products also make rubber moldings and gaskets virtually immune to sun, smog and other deteriorants, their producers say. They are harmless to paints and varnishes, and are colorless.

CLEANING UPHOLSTERY

If your cloth upholstery is soiled, talk to a dry cleaner about cleaning it for you if you remove the trim for him.

Pile fabrics are spruced up with a good vacuum cleaning. The vacuum won't hurt flat fabrics, either. Grease spots come off piles with warm water and soap suds if they haven't been ground in.

Chapter 14 offers more information on cleaning fabrics. Remember, mohair is backed with rubber or substitutes so be careful not to use something that will eat into the backing. Flammable cleaners are to be avoided since they may ignite under brisk rubbing.

Spot removers work well on flat trim spots . . . usually they work *too* well. A normal car has had so much usage and has been exposed to so much light that the color of the upholstery is quite different from what it looked like new. Spot cleaner often leaves the cleansed area standing out with radiant brightness. For this reason, cleaning projects should always include at least the entire section (Fig. 4-4). On boarded trim, such as door panels, avoid saturating the trim so much that it soaks and damages the board.

You may find someone through your dry cleaner or tailor who can reweave very small holes or tears. If just one panel of a seat assembly is

Fig. 4-4. Minor water stains like those found on rear panels of low-mileage 1940 Ford business coupe are best left alone. Faded interior will contrast with cleaned areas.

damaged, it is possible to sew a new section on right over the old one. The new seams, like the old ones, may be hidden by trim bindings.

Mohair often acquires flat spots with age. You may think these are areas where the pile has worn off, but look closely. Sometimes the pile is just flattened. In this case, bring the pile back to attention with a steam treatment.

To steam the pile up, fold a section of cloth, preferably cotton sheeting, into a four-ply piece. Dampen and hold over the flattened area. Gently apply a hot iron to create steam. Do not let the iron lay on the cloth! Remember that rubber backing—it will melt from intense heat. A steam gun can also be used on mohair. Brushing the nap with a whisk broom gives it the right set to blend in with other areas (Fig. 4-5).

CLEANING SOFT TOPS

Older cars with soft top sections are seldom in good condition. If you own one with a serviceable original top insert you should go over it immediately to make sure it will stay that way. Look for cracks or holes that may admit moisture. Clean the top with lukewarm water, using a brush or sponge to loosen dirt. Most top dressings, waxes and cleaners are not healthy for top inserts. New rubber treatments may not hurt them. Some older roof inserts are pyroxylin, an early synthetic rubber. Pyroxylin is very susceptible to cleaning products, so treat it with great caution.

Khaki or "Burbank" cloth convertible tops should be washed with tepid water to remove road grime and spatters. Almost any soap will cause fading. Commercial cleaners can do wonders on vinyl tops but watch out with top dressings and paints. They usually give a very glossy finish, ending up looking something like the shiny tires on the used cars down at Sucker Sam's Bargain Corner.

SPRING REPAIRS

Many times that little old lady who so carefully preserved your car for so many years seems to have grown quite portly in her old age, at least if the spring assemblies are any indication. They may sag and even have a distinct list to one side of the car. Sometimes, but rarely, some of the springs may actually be broken. More often they have either suffered a broken tie or have come unclipped from the edge wire. Repairs may be made easily while you have the cushion assembly out and apart for recovering. Check the resiliency of the springs. If they are just about "dead" and have little remaining temper you should replace them. Check with your local upholsterer for a source of new springs. Springs, like everything it seems, come in a variety of types and qualities so try to match yours as closely as possible. Of course, you might find a cushion in a salvage yard and pirate the good springs from the unworn side of the cushion to patch up yours.

Fig. 4-5. Durable mohair interiors may be brushed and vacuumed to freshen. Strong spot removers may damage rubber backing, though, and should be avoided.

To make spring repairs, remove the worn cushion or back rest assembly. (One exception is the back rest on most 1950s sedans.) Four-doors have a panel that is usually tacked and hog-ringed at the bottom, and can be easily removed or rolled up. On two-doors, you can tip the back rest forward to remove the covering by loosening it at the lower edge. Pre-World War Two cars usually require seat assembly removal.

Once access is gained, the trouble-causing springs can be located. Most 1930s cars have coil springs that are clipped to the perimeter wires and each other. Simply bend the clips open to remove a spring. Replace the coil with one taken from a salvage seat, or ask your local upholsterer if he can get one for you. If you cannot locate a replacement, you can make an effective repair of a weak spring by stretching the spring, then compressing it back into the assembly and reclipping. Some spring assemblies, especially in more expensive cars, have smaller coils, sewn into little pockets. These are known as Marshall springs and the pockets are made by stitching seams into lengths of muslin.

To take up looseness in the original covering, which may have stretched over the years, add an extra layer of cotton felt before reinstalling. Usually, it is advisable to replace the cotton or foam padding since these materials are probably strong contributors to that "old car" smell on warm days. The seat's layer of burlap should also be replaced since burlap has a tendency to dry out and lose strength over the years. It is fairly inexpensive and really should be replaced as a precautionary measure while you have the opportunity, even if it looks okay. A good grade of burlap, with a weight of 10 ounces per square yard of more should be selected for the replacement.

In minor cases of under-padding slippage, untacking the trim at the lower edge and redistributing the padding with a straight edge is possible, using the regulator for final adjustments.

Squeaking springs are easily repaired when you have the seat covering removed. The squeak usually results from coils rubbing against each other. Locate the offenders and isolate them by working some cotton wadding between them.

Chapter 5
Interior Kits—Model "A" to Mustang

One of the hobby's oldest suppliers of antique car interior materials, LeBaron-Bonney Co., of Amesbury, Mass., has marketed a line of complete Model A and early Ford V-8 interior soft trim kits for more than a decade. They have several competitors who, although newer in the field, also supply popular interior restoration kits. Since Model A Fords are undoubtedly the most popular single collector cars, we'll review a kit installation in a typical Model A tudor (Fig. 5-1). Much of the information in this chapter is applicable to any pre-1936 car that has the body framed in wood or uses wood for tacking. Keep in mind, though, the kit installation sequence isn't necessarily the correct program for installation of a made-up interior.

If you want to get involved with a car like a Model A in a very serious way, you should contact an authority on Model As who also is a restoration expert. No other car requires so much authenticity to be a show winner on national club levels. This is because so much documentation has been developed. National Model A Club judges know exactly what style trimming your Model A had when new. They think of cars in *months* and years, instead of just years. You might have a November, 1929 sport coupe, for instance, and its interior might be slightly different from an April, 1929 sport coupe. You'd better know the difference if you're into heavy Model A restoration.

Interior kits are respected in the hobby and they can and have been the basis for national award winning restorations. But much individual initiative is required. Kits come complete with tacks, hog rings, padding and coverings and they are all stitched together for you, so they do save time and dollars. For sprucing up a shabby interior and getting everything nice enough for family tours and local meet competition, the kits are unbeatable just the way they come.

Fig. 5-1. A Model A Ford sedan trimmed with a commercially-available upholstery kit (courtesy LeBaron Bonney Co.).

STRIP OUT FIRST

Before we do the new interior, the old one must be completely undone. Start with the bucket seats and the rear seat assembly. Door panels and rear quarter trim panels are tacked on with brads. Before prying them loose, remove the door handles and window cranks by driving out the pins that secure them. Don't worry about the little trim plates behind them, they are secured from behind. (They are known as escutcheons, by the way.) Also remove the garnish moldings around the windows.

Remove the upper trim panels, which are boarded trim that is tacked and, on some cars, cemented into place. Remove the headliner by untacking it. The tacks are visible now—they were hidden by the upper side trim panels.

When you take off the lower boarded trim, be sure to catch the little springs that go on the crank shafts behind the panels. Put them in a safe place. The small imitation leather panels up under the cowl in front of the door openings are called "kick pads." They are either tacked or screwed on.

The interior kit installation can be started when everything is out of the car. It is a good time to send off the door handles, window cranks and escutcheon plates to the plater. Be sure you know what finish they originally had. The escutcheons come off from behind and have prongs that bend over to cinch them to a specially-shaped washer on the back of the panel board. Put the escutcheon washers up with the handle springs.

BEGINNING THE RESTORATION

Start replacing the interior with the new headliner. Begin tacking at the rear bow, the last upper one, not the one at the top of the rear window frame. The fabric will eventually be tacked there, too, though, so leave enough for this.

Following the instructions that come with the kit, start next at the center bow, tacking out to the edges from the center. Make sure your headliner is centered, too. Not every bow will have a corresponding listing strip. You can mark the correct ones as you remove the old headliner, or look for tack holes. At the windshield header and rear window frame, allow a bit of looseness. The upper boarded trim panels will take it up for you. Check the fit by holding these pieces up to the headliner, adjust as required and drive the tacks home.

Windlacing

Windlace is that nice-looking, heavy fabric or leatherette-covered cord that finishes off the edges around door openings (Fig. 5-2). It isn't really right to say it finishes it off, though, since it actually goes on first. Start with the vertical strips. Cut off about ½-inch of tubing at the top after you've tacked the windlace onto the door pillar by the tacking strip. Make a flap out of the empty cloth and fold it over, tacking it in place. The horizontal strips are run across next, being carefully placed so they are absolutely straight. This time an inch of the rubber core is removed and the resulting flap is tacked over the one made from the vertical strip. On cars where the windlace can round a curved corner, slit the selvedge tacking strip ninety degrees to the tubing at close intervals to give it "bend."

The windlace is really an inner seal for the door opening. Its job is to keep out wind, dust, and moisture. It should be aligned with this in mind. Adjust it so it snugs right up over the cracks between the doors and body pillars when the doors are shut. However, don't let it bind or get squeezed in the cracks.

Windlace strips on the cowl pillars may be held with clips or by metal trim moldings, or a combination of both with a few tacks thrown in for good measure. Let the disassembly be your guide.

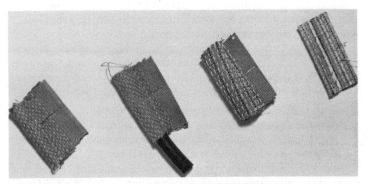

Fig. 5-2. Common styles of windlace and trim binding are still available from interior restoration supply houses. Windlace, or windhose has rubber tubing core, as visible in sample second from left.

Trim Panels

Next is the installation of boarded trim panels. Except for door panels, boarded trim is usually attached with brads. The brads are driven right through the fabric until heads are flush. Then a regulator or large needle is used to open the weave of the fabric and slip it over the brad head.

Door panels install with clips and one screw at each lower corner. Don't forget to install the escutcheon plates before putting on door panels. Remember those little springs that go behind the panels, too. Install the kick pads in the proper manner. If they are partially held by screws, use the correct plated screw with recessed washers. The leatherette kick pads are held on with screws. Carefully align them.

New Seat Covering

Covering the seats is done out of the car. You can work on your table or on a clean throw spread on the floor. Remove all the old padding, layer by layer. If the old padding is good, build it up by filling obvious depressions with cotton felt. For a really good and odor-free job you should replace it.

If you strip the seats down to the springs, now is the time to make spring repairs. You can paint the springs with primer or paint to stop rusting.

Start re-upholstering the spring assembly with a layer of burlap. Lay it over the springs so an equal amount hangs over on all sides. Fold the burlap over the trim wire and use the hog rings that come with the kit to ring it to the coil springs at their first turn. Don't hog ring right to the rim wire as this will cause abrasive bumps. Draw the burlap tight and work to the next corner, then go all around the wire ringing every other coil.

To cover the backrest spring assembly, lay it flat on your work surface. Center the cotton and denim layers as you did the burlap and ring it in the same manner. Draw the denim down tightly so it compresses the cotton. You can work the cotton padding around by whacking and pushing after it is covered, to get a good, even surface (Fig. 5-3).

The front bucket seat coverings have a forming panel sewn into the pre-assembled unit. As you draw it over the backrest, feel with your finger for the clip it engages. Turn the bottom of the back part of the covering under the tack into the wood strip at the spring assembly base.

Four welt strips will hang down from the assembly after you've tacked as described. They are extensions of the cord that runs along the seams. Pull the back strips straight down until the welting is good and snug across the top of the assembly. Check to make sure it is straight, too. Then turn the end of the welt under and tack to the wooden tack strip. These welt cords were often originally held in place by a tack through a piece of Ford scrap. It may be a very good sample of the top material originally used on the top material originally used on the car.

Pull the front welt strips down across the bottom of the spring assembly, until they are snug against the hinge arm. Tuck the lower edge of the side panel in as you tack.

To complete, draw the bottom edge of the front panel down and around the spring base, tacking it securely. If these welt strips stick out, cut them off.

Seat Cushions

Seat cushions are covered with burlap as described, but a sisal pad is used over it and under the cotton felt instead of denim. Center the materials and ring them in place. Turn the covering assembly inside-out and fit the upper seam to the top of the rim wire. It should fit exactly (Fig. 5-4). Assuming it does, roll the edges down and fit it to the spring assembly. Tilt the cushion to stand on its back edge, center again, and tack into the rabbeted strip on the upper area of the cushion rein.

Working the covering down as you go, and keeping a close eye on alignment, tack the sides back to about six inches from the rear. Then shift the cushion and tack the back.

Pull the loose part of the panel down snug against the metal hinge arm and across the back, overlapping the back panel as much as you can. Tack the end, then the rest of the side panel. Now, set the complete seat assembly up in the normal position, folding the backrest forward. Lay the hinge panel (supplied) on the back of the backrest with the wide end lined

Fig. 5-3. Model A Ford seat springs have been stripped of old upholstery and painted. New upholstery installation begins with layers of burlap, padding and denim. Hog-rings secure under layers to spring assembly.

up to the base of the cushion. Tack the stitched end of the panel envelope into the tacking strip. Turning the seat assembly up, flip the hinge panel over and bring the other end down under the seat base, tacking to the rabbet. A rabbet, by the way, is simply a groove, provided for tacks. To finish, turn the seat assembly clear over and tack the seat bottom panel into place, then replace the necessary hardware.

Rear Backrest

The backrest spring assembly, or upper portion of the back seat, is similar to other operations. Burlap and cotton felt are installed first. The covering has a denim flap at the lower edge which should be lined up as you work the covering over the assembly. Like the front seat backrest covering, you roll the covering inside out and then unroll it into place.

Pull the covering down tight and stay-tack at all corners. Then rotate the assembly so you can easily pull the bottom panel down and tack it into the rabbet provided. Space tacks at ¾- to 1¼-inch intervals.

Center the covering to the top frame and line up, then turn the assembly over so lower edge is near you. Reach across the assembly, grasping material at top center and pulling over springs and down to rabbet slot in top of the framework. Then turn the backrest over to the usual position and slap and work the fabric into shape.

Turn the assembly over again and pull the top edge over to the rabbet again. Tack each end, check the whole thing, and then space tacks across at three inch intervals. You might run out of tacks but an interior restorer suggests that a tack an inch is better yet. Work the surface and keep drawing tension on the assembly as you go. Watch the seams to keep them straight. Retack at the center if you have to.

A draw string is sewn into each end of the fabric. Tack one end of the string to the bottom wood frame piece, over the fabric. Tack right through the knot into the rabbet. Pull the other end of the cord, gathering material into puckers as it is taken up. Draw the cord as tight as it will go without distorting the front edge of the spring assembly, then stay tack it to the rabbet near the end of the top part of the wood frame. Lash a turn around the tack and drive it home. Drive another tack through the cord, then trim off excess.

Rear Seat Cushion

Covering the rear full-width cushion assembly is similar to all cushions that are assembled with a wood frame or have wood tacking strips.

On the cushion an insulating pad is added over the burlap, followed by cotton felt, all hog-ringed into place. Roll the cover up so it is inside-out and fit it to the edge wire of the spring assembly, making sure it matches up. Roll the edges down over the assembly, centering as you do so. Carefully line up the pleats and welting by whacking and working the covering with your hands.

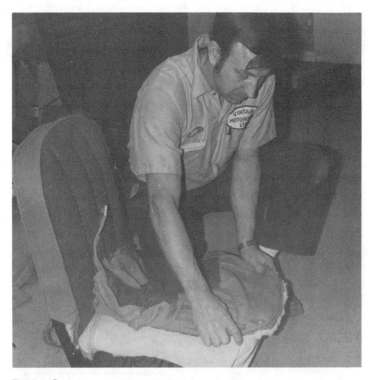

Fig. 5-4. Covering material is turned inside out for fitting to spring cushion, then is rolled down into place.

Turn the unit over, bottom up, and push down any cotton that may be peering over the edge of the frame. Stay tack at the front edge centering the border trim to the assembly. Tack in about an inch from the edge. Do the front corners in the same manner, then draw side borders towards the back and stay tack(Fig. 5-5). Align as needed, then drive home the front tacks. Draw and stretch the covering straight back and stay-tack ends to within six inches of each corner.

The welting comes out beyond the side pieces. Turn the cushion right side up and draw the ends around the rear corners of the assembly, pulling tight. Hog-ring them to the rim wire just around the corner. If everything is lined up, finish stay tacking and tack end panels to base. Go back to the end of the rear panel and turn the corners where you left the six inches untacked. Tack out to the end and close the corner with a hog ring through the fold on each end (Fig. 5-6).

Each upholstery kit comes with its own instructions and the installer should follow them closely. Now you know what to expect at least! Leather kits are similar, except the boarded trim uses binding to cover tacks.

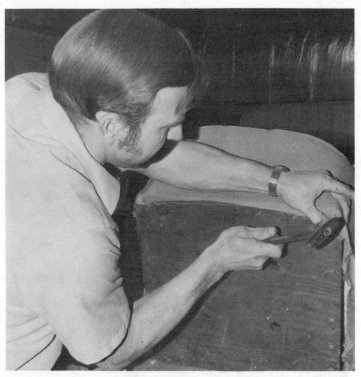

Fig. 5-5. Upholstery covering is stay-tacked at corners. Padding is adjusted and covering is carefully aligned before final tacking.

MUSTANG INTERIOR KIT

Jim Willems, chief instructor for McPherson College's automotive restoration school, has used a number of kits in the restoration of 1965-66 Mustangs and finds that the kits generally fit well (Figs. 5-7, 5-8). The author asked him to point out areas that have caused trouble for students using the kits.

"You should check out the springs—which are almost always in good condition," Willems says. The trouble is likely to begin with the foam rubber padding between the springs and the cover.

"If your old cover is in extremely poor condition and some of the rubber padding is ruined, find another seat rather than attempt a repair. Like all late model cars, the Mustang has a molded rubber cushion. If you stuff cotton in there it will turn out lumpy. If the cushion is torn to any extent, find a good used seat.

"In the case of a Mustang the right and left seats interchange, so you will find that the drivers seat usually will catch more wear than the right hand seat, and you can use the cushion from a right side to repair a driver's seat. You just use the rubber cushion, the frame is different."

Fig. 5-6. Panel which attaches to folding seat bottom on Model A 2-door phaeton is original, varies slightly from version supplied with kit. Such details are important to national car club meet judges, may be insignificant in average restoration.

Willems warned that upgrading a standard Mustang interior to an embossed, optional "Pony" interior entails using different cushions than those under standard seat covers. You will have to obtain some Pony cushions, which to date are not reproduced, although the Pony covers are.

As in all interior work, it is important to center a Mustang seat cover before beginning the installation. The bucket seat covers appear to be too

Fig. 5-7. Coming on strong in the collector car market, the Mustang charges ahead in availability of reproduction interior parts and trim.

03148 Moulding-W/S Outside-Belt
C5ZZ-6503148-B 65/68 ... 13.90

04104 Sun Visor-Less Arm & Brkt.

C6ZZ-7604104-DAJ

C5ZZ-6504104-EFC 65/66, (63, 65) White ... 23.15
C6ZZ-7604104-DAJ 65/66, (76), Black ... 23.85

04114 Pin-Visor Anchor
C3DZ-7604114-B 66/69, includes rubber tip ... 1.60

04115 Rubber Tip-Visor Pin
D1DZ-6204115-A 65/66 ... .64

04290 Padded Dash

C5ZZ-6504290-AFB

C6ZZ-6504290-BAB

C5ZZ-6504290-AFB 65, Blue ... 110.95
C5ZZ-6504290-AFD 65, Red ... 110.95
C5ZZ-6504290-AFA 65, Black ... 110.95
C6ZZ-6504290-BAD 66, Blue ... 110.95
C6ZZ-6504290-BAC 66, Burgundy ... 110.95
C6ZZ-6504290-BAB 66, Black ... 110.95
C7ZZ-6504292-AIA 67/68, Instrument panel, lower ... 15.05
C9ZZ-6504282-AIA 69/70, Black. w o integral air cond ... 159.30
C9ZZ-6504282-BIA 69/70, Black. w integral air cond ... 159.30
D0ZZ-6504282-A 69/70, Blue. w o integral air cond ... 159.30
D0ZZ-6504282-D 69/70, Blue. w-integral air cond ... 159.30
D1ZZ-6504282-E 71/72, Green, less mldg. on forward edge ... 102.15
D3ZZ-6504282-A 73, Black. ... 171.15
D3ZZ-6504282-B 73, Blue ... 171.15
D3ZZ-6504282-C 73, Avorado ... 171.15
D3ZZ-6504282-E 73, Ginger ... 171.15

04774 Panel - Instrument Panel - Center

C7ZZ-6504774-B 67/68, Camera case ... 4.50
C9ZZ-6504774-B 69/70, Blk, Corinthian grain with radio. Exc 63C, 65E ... 13.00
C9ZZ-6504774-F 69/70, (63C, 65E), dark teakwood with radio, from 1-6/69 ... 20.55
D1DZ-6304774-C 71/73, (63D, R, 65F), ginger, black - wood grain finsh. used with gauges ... 20.30
D1ZZ-6504774-A 71/73 (63D, R, 65D, 76D), ginger, black - camera case finish, used w/o gauges with Mustang nameplate ... 20.30
D1ZZ-650774-L 71/73 (63D, 65D, 76D), ginger, black - camera case finish, used with gauges ... 20.30

06010 Glove Compartment
C5ZZ-6506010-A 65/66 ... 6.15

060A12 Bezel, Glove Compt. Door
C6OZ-C2060A12-A 67/68 ... 1.00

06064 Catch-Glove Compt. Door Latch
C5ZZ-6506064-A 65/66 (63B, 65B, 76B) ... 1.15
C6DZ-6206064-A 67/68 ... .72

06072 Latch-Glove Compt. Non Locking
C6DZ-6206072-B 67/68, Instrument panel ... 4.70

10130 Label-Sill Plate
S7MS-6310130-A 65/70, GT 350/500 ... 1.50

10176-7 Rocker Panel Moulding
C5ZZ-6510176-A 65/66, RH ... 35.20
C5ZZ-6510177-A 65/66, LH ... 35.20
C7ZZ-6510176-A 67/68, RH ... 20.50
C7ZZ-6510177-A 67/68, LH ... 20.50

10316 Regulator Ass'y.-Alternator
D9PZ-10316-A 65/73 ... 20.55

10346 Alternator Ass'y. New Write or phone for price & availability

10346 Alternator, Rebuilt (Exchange) Write or phone for availability and price

10718 Clamp - Battery Hold Down

C2DZ-10718-A 65-66, with Std. Battery ... 1.65
C2DZ-10718-A 65-66, with H.D. Battery ... 1.75
C5AZ-10718-A 67-73 ... 1.30

10732 Tray, Battery
C5ZZ-10732-C 65/66, all batteries ... 6.35
C7ZZ-10732-D 67/68, all batteries ... 12.85

10756 Bolt, Battery
D4SZ-10756-A 67/68 ... 1.25

10780 Member-Rear Floor Cross-Rear
C5ZZ-7610780-B 65/70 ... 17.55

10804 Regulator-Instrument Voltage
B9MZ-10804-C 65/66 ... 6.20
C6DZ-10804-A 67/68 ... 4.95

10838 Housing-Instrument Cluster

C5ZZ-10838-A C5ZZ-10838-B
C6ZZ-10838-A C7ZZ-10838-C
C7ZZ-10838-B C8ZZ-10838-A
C8ZZ-10838-B

C5ZZ-10838-A 65, with idiot lites only ... 20.70
C5ZZ-10838-B 65/66, wood grain finish - use with clusters with ammeter & oil pressure gauges ... 20.70
C6ZZ-10838-A 66, Black camera case finish - use only on clusters with ammeter & oil pressure gauge ... 20.70
C7ZZ-10838-C 67, (63A, 65A, 65C, 76A, 76C) Black camera case finish ... 18.40
C7ZZ-10838-B 67, (63B, 65B, 76B) Brushed alum. ... 32.65
C8ZZ-10838-A 68, Camera case ... 32.65
C8ZZ-10838-B Wood grain ... 32.65

10850 Ammeter-Instrument Cluster
C5ZZ-10850-A 65 ... 9.45
C6ZZ-10850-A 66 ... 13.80
C7ZZ-10850-A 67/68, (less tach) (except GT 350/500) ... 15.10

10852 Member-Front Floor Cross
C7ZZ-6510852-B 67/70 ... 29.60

10883 Gauge-Instrument Temp.
C5ZZ-10883-B 65/66, used only on clusters with charge indicator ... 9.45

10884 Sender-Water Temp. Sender
Specify year & type engine ... 4.95

11002 Starter, Rebuilt (Exchange) Write or phone for availability and price

11218-9 Pan-Rear Floor
C9ZZ-6511218-A 65/70 RH ... 26.70
C9ZZ-6511219-A 65/70 LH ... 26.70

Fig. 5-8. Page from Mustang supplier's catalog. Padded dash pads, sun visors, instrument cluster housings are shown. Door panels, carpet kits, seat cover kits and hundreds of other items are also available (courtesy Larry's Mustang Parts).

tight to the beginner, but, assures Willems, they will fit. Some restorers have found that it is easier to get the cover on the backrest by "rolling" it on like a sock. Jim Willems suggests using a bit of talcum powder to facilitate the installation. He stresses that the cover must be pulled down all the way, yet warns that one should not pull too hard on the sides since some students have ripped covers by pulling on them.

Ringing Down The Insert

"It is extremely important to get the insert ringed down," Jim Willems says as he explains how the backrest cover goes on a Mustang bucket seat. "You have to run a wire in the tube sewed for it—the wire fits through this sleeve and must be stapled or hog-ringed down before going any further. If it isn't aligned correctly it will have an irregular appearance. It is important to get it centered." The wire goes down through the rubber to the spring assembly, and is the basis of a good installation. Willems says of most sloppy-looking jobs, "It is simply that they didn't get the insert down right—this is the most difficult part."

How Much Time?

A complete interior kit might be installed in a Mustang over the weekend. Jim Willems estimates a beginning upholsterer could install a molded carpet kit in 3-4 hours. This entails removing seats, the old carpet (held down by screws), kick panels and shifter console. Another 3-4 hours might be expended installing the new seat covers on the front buckets, and perhaps two more will be spent installing the back seat's covering.

"After the carpet is in and there are no holes for the seat fasteners they can easily be located by pushing an ice pick up from under the floor," Willems says. "These holes should definitely be cut," he adds, "A hole in the carpet can be either a round hole cut a little oversize or simply an X cut in the right place." Don't try to set the seat in place and start the bolt through; it will probably catch a thread and make a very visible run in your new carpet.

Willems says that on a full interior restoration he begins reassembly with the installation of the instrument pad, followed by the headliner (on coupes). Window adjustments and new quarter trim is taken care of before the carpet is installed to save wear and tear on the new carpets. The seats, of course are removed from the car for recovering and they are usually the last thing to go back into the interior. Door trim panels can easily be installed during a lull in the action near the end of the project.

Chapter 6
The Mysterious Headliner

Headliners, especially on older cars, are a mystery to many people. They just hang there. Push on a headliner and you cannot feel any connection between it and the steel or wood roof bows.

Many times the headliner is the last survivor of the original interior since it is largely up and out of the way. But even then it probably has water stains, small holes and is very soiled from smoke and time. Certainly you will at least want to remove it for cleaning.

Most often, though, the headliner is worn, tattered and otherwise deteriorated and you will want to replace it. Moths love headliners, too . . . you should keep this in mind when you install your new one. Mice have an instinctive urge to chew holes in the headliner. They stand on the sun visor boards to do this. Look above when buying a car; and fold the visors down when storing your car to prevent this sort of damage.

Surprisingly, replacing a headliner isn't a terribly difficult job. On older cars with flat, square headliners you can buy headliner cloth and make your own without a hassle. The secret of the headliner is its "listing strips" sewn onto the back with a special machine that doesn't put the thread all the way through the headliner cloth. The headliner hangs from these strips with ½- or ¼-inch clearance from the bows (Fig. 6-1).

To make a headliner requires careful measuring. To do a quick job, figure how deep the listings would be, then lay the fabric out and make a line at the bow. Measure out and make a line at the bow. Measure out enough on each side of the line to make the listing's depth, then stitch a seam across the fold. The stitches will be visible, but not very much, since they are horizontal when the headliner is installed. To do the job right, ask at area tailor shops for a "blind sewing" machine. They are used to stitch pants cuffs. A shop may install listings for you.

Fig. 6-1. Model A Ford headliner is attached by listing to bows and is stapled at rear. Boarded trim panels will cover rough edges.

Some early cars, usually expensive jobs, had real leather headliners. These were usually made in individual sections, tacked directly to the bows without listings. Seaming cord was used to cover tacks and joints.

Most conventional cars had cloth and unless yours is a really odd machine or a convertible, of course, chances are one of the suppliers in our appropriate appendix can fix you up with a pre-cut headliner cloth with listing strips attached. They are quite reasonable and are well worth the time saved in making patterns and stitching.

If a car has wooden bows and a roof insert, take care of any water leaks before installing the new headliner.

REMOVE THE OLD, CENTER THE NEW

To remove the headliner on older cars, first remove the boarded trim upper panels on the sides and at the rear. Many cars have a panel above the windshield opening, too. To get these panels off you will probably have to remove window garnish moldings. Be careful in removing the panels as they are often both tacked and cemented in place. Mark the tack holes as you loosen the old headliner along the edges. This will help position the new one.

If making your own headliner, pay close attention to which bows have listing strips and which do not as you are removing the old liner.

Center the new headliner by folding it in half and stay-tack at the exact center of the front bow. Work out to the edges, stay-tacking, so you can work out wrinkles and draws later. You will have special fun doing this if the fabric has stripes or designs in it that need to be aligned, too. Keep the headliner tight and smooth.

On some cars there will be a trim binding to cover the line where the boarded trim encounters the headliner. Install it carefully, fitting the boarded trim up to make sure it is straight. A back panel, often with molded cardboard backing, and a panel above the windshield usually cover the rough edges on pre-1936 cars.

Later cars use the windshield garnish moldings and the rear package tray to cover the edges, eliminating the extra boarded trim panels.

LISTING WIRES DESIGNS

During the mid-1930s many manufacturers switched to listing wires to hang headliners, eliminating most tacking. The change was the result of bodies becoming nearly all steel with full, metal panel roof sections.

The listing wires were small gauge tension wires sized to span the top opening fitting into slots along the sides. They were usually wrapped in waxed paper to prevent damp rust coming through the listing cloth and soiling the headliner cloth. The waxed paper trick didn't always work and we've all seen cars with rust stains speading out away from lines on the headliner. This is seepage from above.

On some cars, the listing wires clip into the steel bows, fitting into clips stamped into the bows. The listing pockets had holes to allow this on original headliners.

Listing wires on a car will be of varied lengths. You can save time and trouble later by marking a number (remember which way you're counting!) on masking tape and labeling each one as you remove it in numerical sequence.

Car bodies that have headliners rolling down to the package shelf often used the last few rear listing wires to form the headliner, too. These are heavier wire and are usually secured with screws at their ends. Sometimes, though, they pop out when flexed. Take a good look before ripping out.

A TYPICAL GENERAL MOTORS INSTALLATION

Removing and installing a headliner on a late 1930s GM car is similar to the operation on any car with a cloth headliner so we'll review the job on one of these.

Start by removing the sun visors (the inside, fabric-covered type). Then, remove your domelight cover, being especially careful not to put your finger through the plastic lens. On other makes the cover may be held by screws, or it may twist off—be gentle. Remove the domelight switch and its escutcheon if it is attached to the headliner cloth and remove other trim items such as hanger posts and assist straps.

Blend down the wire-on molding along the side roof rails to reveal headliner tacks. This molding is right above the windlace. Remove tacks with a suitable tool. Pull out the back seat assembly if you haven't already done so and remove the package shelf. This will expose more tacks holding the rear edge of the headliner cloth, which may also be cemented in place. Remove it carefully.

On coupe bodies, it may be necessary to remove the rear side window garnish moldings before dropping the headliner. On all cars, remove the windshield garnish molding frame, loosening tacks and cement beneath.

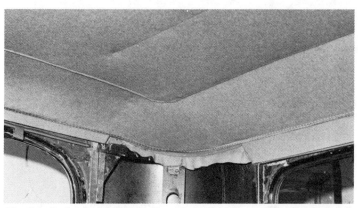

Fig. 6-2. Packard sedan's headliner is much more complex than Model A. Pressed-fiber board formers give curve to perimeters, welting finishes edges. Boarded trim will fit flush with welting, must be carefully aligned.

Beginning at the front, start removing the listing wires, stacking the headliner accordion fashion as you go. Bend down tabs on the bows with needle nose pliers. Don't panic if a few break off, you can easily fashion new ones with self-tapping screws. Don't forget: The rear-most listings, if they help form the headliner, may be screwed into place.

IN GOES THE NEW

Installing the new headliner is mostly a reversal of the removal. Clean and paint the listing wires with a rust-preventative coating. Just to make sure, wrap them in wax paper again. Slide the listing wires into the correct pocket and, working rear to front, install them. Depending on the car, you may start the headliner at the windshield or at the lower edge of the roof in the rear, if it isn't similar to the job we're talking about.

Listing wires either flex into place or, if they have offset ends, may be put in by tilting rearward, slipping into the proper notches and rotating forward to lock them in. Center the cloth by using the domelight opening as a reference.

Cars have either a tacking strip or formed clips for attaching the cloth on the sides. A flat special headlining tool, similar in appearance to a putty knife, is used to force the fabric over the clips. Cement the cloth as the original was at the appropriate places.

Even 1950s cars have headliners essentially like the pre-war cars. Once exception is the hardtop with chrome roof bows. This has cardboard strips glued to the vinyl headliner. These strips slip into channels on the back of the bows. This is a hard job so stock up on patience before you start. The bows are adjustable at the sides and you can get just the right amount of "fullness" with a little work. When satisfied with the hang of the vinyl, secure the screws on the bows and tuck in the edges with a headliner tool (Fig. 6-2).

Chapter 7
Trim Assemblies

Until the mid-1930s, most cars had seat frames made out of wood. Then around 1935 some metal found its way into the assemblies. By the time World War II was over, wood had all but vanished from seat assemblies.

SPRING ASSEMBLIES

Spring assemblies were relatively simple and used two basic types of springs. The most common on volume produced cars were spiral springs of differing lengths. They were made with a wood frame at the bottom and a wire frame at the top. The springs were attached to the frame and bound together with clips at the top.

Most expensive cars often used so-called Marshall spring assemblies. These were made up of smaller, lighter springs, sewn into individual compartments, then sewn to wire frames at top and bottom. Seat backrest assemblies are usually constructed similarly but use lighter weight springs.

The seat assembly consists of the frame, spring assemblies, upholstering and the hardware used for attaching it to the car's floor. A complete seat assembly can be made for cars that used mostly wood for construction but it is a job for an expert unless you have a very early car with very simple seat cushions on a wood frame. These can be duplicated using home furniture techniques and equipment (Fig. 7-1).

Removing Spring Assemblies

Until around 1940, you could usually remove cushion spring assemblies without removing the seat frame and adjustment mechanism. Then it became necessary to remove the entire assembly. If your car has a

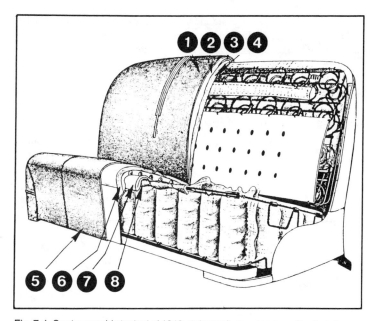

Fig. 7-1. Seat assembly typical of 1940-style medium-price cars. Back rest uses coil type spring assembly, cushion has "Marshall" springs in muslin pockets. 1) Back rest cover cloth. 2) Less burlap cotton pad. 3) Cotton batting, 7½-oz., 5½-inch wide, straddles top border wire. 4) Burlap pad. 5) Cover cloth; hog ring rubber pad skirt to bottom border wire; turn and tack through cloth and rubber pad skirt to bottom of seat frame, using 4-oz. Swede tacks spaced one inch apart. 6) Foam rubber pad; hog-ring rubber pad skirt to bottom border wire at back of spring; tacked with cover cloth at bottom of seat frame. 7) Cotton batting, 56 inches long, one third opened; placed over jute roll on front border wire. 8) Jute roll is attached with hog rings around top border wire, using 17 hog rings equally spaced.

unit seat assembly you should check a shop manual for instructions on removing it. It can be tricky since various methods were used to attach the assembly and put tension on the seat adjuster springs.

If no information exists or is available to you, make the side trim panels loose on the lower edges of the seat. Usually the adjuster handle has to be removed, too. Carefully examine the assembly to determine how to remove it. Some cars, 1940 Buicks for example, can give you a nasty zap with the adjuster spring if you aren't careful. While you have the assembly out on the bench is a good time to adjust and repair the latch and track assemblies. If your car has a hydraulic seat adjuster, you should carefully inspect it for leaks or corrosion. Just to be safe, it really should be rebuilt at this time, and new hydraulic connections installed.

To strip a cushion assembly on a pre-war car, turn it upside down and remove the tacks from the wood frame. If the upholstery has buttons, release the bent-over arms holding them to the spring wires and pull them out. Roll up the outer covering and undo the under-padding which will be tacked or hog-ringed. Loosen the spring wire assembly by undoing the fasteners or leather strips attaching it to the wood drame. Now is the time to do service work on the springs, realigning them and painting them. Rusted spring assemblies may be sandblasted to remove all traces of rust and painted with a rust-resistant paint.

Removing Whole Seat Assemblies

On cars that require removal of the entire seat assembly the cushion is held by clips under the front upholstery skirt. Untack it and undo the clips. Many cars of this era had stationary rear seat backs. A wire-on molding or a strip of Randall molding usually finishes off the upper edge on these cars. Remove the Randall molding or open the wire-on type to reveal

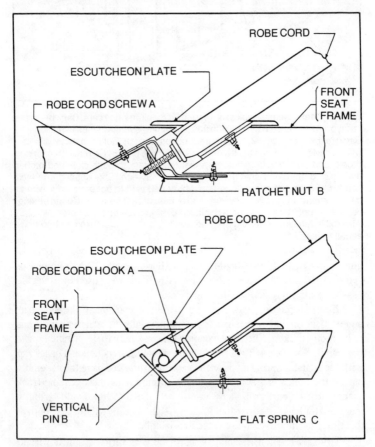

Fig. 7-2. Two methods of attaching robe cords to rear of front seat back rest assembly.

Fig. 7-3. Trim assemblies in typical 1940-style 2-door sedan. 1) Tacking strip. 2) Cardboard foundation. 3) Blue wadding—cemented to foundation board. 4) Quarter panel material; anchored to door opening by binding strip; at window opening by being turned over cardboard foundation and cemented; tacked at corners with 2½ oz. Swede tacks spaced at two-inch intervals; tacked at rear edge with 2½-oz. Swede tacks spaced every two inches; bottom is turned over and cemented. 5) Windhose or windlace, tacked to tacking strip with 6-oz. Swede tacks every two inches. 6) Dust cloth seamed to cover cloth. 7) Cardboard arm rest foundation board. 8) Blue wadding—cemented to foundation. 9) Cover cloth; plain seamed to dust cloth; turned over foundation, cemented and tacked with 2½-oz. Swede tacks every two inches; turned into ashtray recess and cemented to wood. 10) Wood frame. 11) Cotton pad, placed on foundation board as shown. 12) Silencer pad made of blue wadding, cemented to metal.

tacks. Then remove the covering as is typical of the operation described for earlier cars. When putting it back together remember to keep the tacks along the upper edge in a straight line so they will be covered by the molding (Fig. 7-2).

Boarded trim, such as door and quarter panels, is usually cemented to the board by folding over the edge and cementing or otherwise attaching on the back. Sometimes the fabric is stitched, too. Some cars have curved upper rear panels that are difficult to reproduce if they are damaged, so take care when removing them. Most backing board is made of fiberboard (Fig. 7-3).

Making Spring Assemblies

If the seat cushion or backrest on your antique is missing completely, don't despair. You can manufacture a new one yourself. You will probably need a pattern to go by (some early car and truck cushions are so simple that you can make a good cushion by using the seat retainer frame as a basic pattern and building up from there).

Spring edge wire is used to form the outer edges of the spring assembly. A special tool for bending this wire can be made from a short length of ¼-inch diameter soft metal pipe. You thread the spring wire through the pipe, then bend it with a quick flick of your wrist, attempting to produce a curve in the wire of an angle a bit tighter than needed. Bend the wire back out to the desired angle.

You can make a spring wire bending jig with a little imagination if you are short on dexterity, or even use your regular hammer and garage vise to get corners shaped. Springs can be purchased from an upholstery supplier (probably through your local upholsterer) or salvaged from another similar seat assembly. They should approximate the original type and be fastened to the edge wire in the original manner. However, you do have a bit more latitude here than in some areas—few judges remove a seat cushion and knock down points for non-authentic springs. Not to say that it *couldn't* happen, though! Remember when selecting springs that the number of coils in a spring increases proportionately with its cost and efficiency. You can make yourself a little more comfortable in your low-cost car by installing a better grade of seat springs, perhaps.

ARM RESTS

Often the only part needing work on a low mileage car interior is the arm rests. They are rather mysterious so we'll review several common styles (Fig. 7-4).

A typical 1930-style, plain armrest uses a wood block foundation with a layer of cotton wadding under the upholstery cloth. This type of arm rest is usually held on with screws through a metal trim plate on the reverse side of the panel. You will have to remove the door or quarter panel to take the arm rest off.

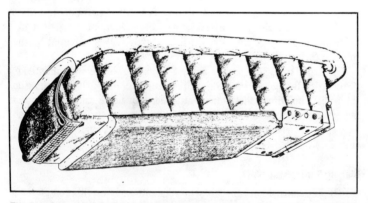

Fig. 7-4. Spring construction of a rear seat center arm rest from an early 1940s sedan. In essence, a miniature cushion using Marshall springs.

Fig. 7-5. 1938 Cadillac 60-S used leather upper face on arm rest, and across upper door panel.

Usually there is a curved seam at the front edge of a plain arm rest. Hopefully, you can determine the location of this seam from the old upholstery and make your pattern from it. Using a scrap from the new upholstery, if available, stitch the necessary seam, then cover the wood block and new cotton wadding, tacking the fabric around on the back edge of the wood. Re-attach with the original metal plate and screws.

Higher-priced sedans often had fancy, pleated arm rests. These are really miniature cushion assemblies with a wood frame, coil springs, stuffed pleats and buttons. They are usually blind stitched at the front edge and tacked along the bottom skirt. After loosening, a screw is removed at the rear and the arm rest is lifted off a hook in the panel at the front (Fig. 7-5).

A pleated arm rest construction has a block of wood for a foundation covered with cotton wadding. Over it four or more spiral springs, held with cloth or leather strips, are placed and covered with burlap, tacked with tension drawn on the springs to form the contour. More wadding is sewn over the burlap, sometimes as many as six layers of wadding are used. The covering itself is a complex piece of sewing, and hopefully the old one can be used for a pattern. Tacks are used to pull in the pleats at the right spots, then they are covered with button-headed tacks to finish.

The center arm rest in cars with back seat assemblies is another miniature cushion assembly. Usually you have to remove the back rest assembly to loosen the arm rest.

During the late 1930s, the use of molded sponge rubber, or foam, to fill and form arm rests became popular. These were made by cementing the filler right to a metal panel contoured to form the arm rest. Most of these attach with two screws angled up under the assembly. Some have one screw and a slip-over clip.

Sponge-rubber arm rests were covered with upholstery cloth, often using a leatherette insert for a wear pad. Seaming cord is usually used to cover the seams that are sewn along the upper edge. On many cars, the metal panel was attached to a wood tacking block. Use the trim regulator to locate the screw holes.

DOOR POCKETS

Door pockets were once popular. Very early cars had flaps sewn into the door panel trim and large pockets used for storage of tools, maps and such. Later, pockets were fitted with elastic strips across the upper lip to keep them taut. Panel board was used to make these pockets and they were completely assembled before installation (Fig. 7-6).

Door pockets are easily made if the old one is present for use as a pattern. After they are finished, they are sewn to the door panel cloth.

DECORATED TRIM PANELS

Many trim panels have raised lines accenting decorative designs. This was accomplished by using rubber or cane half-round strips which were called "trim risers."

Fig. 7-6. Door pockets with shirred openings are made up as complete units, then sewn to panels.

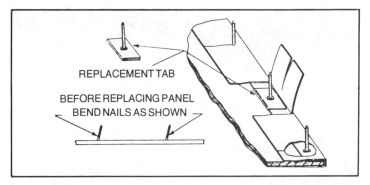

REPLACEMENT TAB

BEFORE REPLACING PANEL
BEND NAILS AS SHOWN

Fig. 7-7. Door trim pads are often fastened with simple nails on a binding strip cemented under the turned-over panel cloth. Replacement tabs, as shown, can be easily fashioned.

If starting all over with new foundation board, draw the lines for the risers right on the board. If possible, salvage the risers from the old boards. They aren't readily available, so you will have to improvise to make new ones. Any half-round strip of the right width will do although it helps if it is a material through which a tack can be driven. The trim risers are cemented to the foundation board (Fig. 7-7). On cars with wood panels the trim risers sometimes had a tacking strip attached to their flat sides, or were tacked right through. Before installing the new covering, the trim risers are thoroughly covered with trim cement. Then the fabric is carefully formed over the risers, making sure it is struck down evenly all along both edges of the strip. For insurance, a heavy duty sewing machine capable of sewing through the trim board is used to sew the edges (Fig. 7-8).

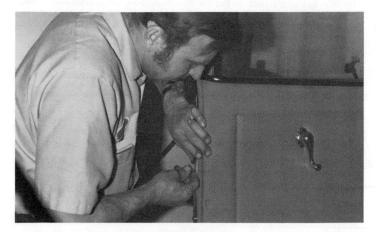

Fig. 7-8. On cars with boarded trim that is nailed to wood framework with brads, a trim regulator or large needle is used to slip the upholstery weave over the head of the brad after it is driven flush with panel.

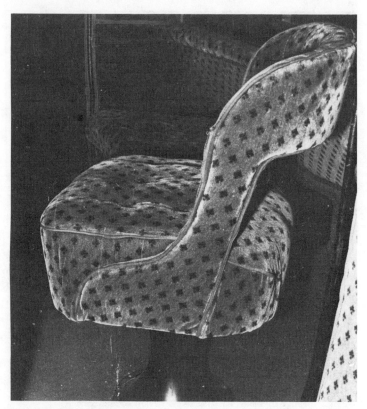

Fig. 7-9. Early cars, such as this electric coupe were upholstered with furniture maker's methods. And you thought swivel seats were new?

SEAT BUTTONS

Two types of buttons are found on seat assemblies. The most common button is the prong type. It has slender, flat prongs that are pushed through the locating hole in the upholstery covering. The manner of attaching is just like a clasp envelope. The prongs go through a washer and are bent out to secure the button. Some buttons have short prongs and the washers are placed behind the layers of padding. Others are fastened at the back of the cushion assembly. By compressing the springs, then bending the prongs over the washer, the buttons can be used to hold tension on the surface, drawing in pleats for added effect.

On cars with deep pleats, a stronger method is used to attach the buttons so they will compress the springs. A coil spring wire, similar to a common door spring, runs across the bottom or back of the spring assembly along the same level as the buttons. A length of chain or wire is ringed to this spring for each button. Then, using a T-handled tool, with a hook on the end, the upholsterer works through the assembly from the

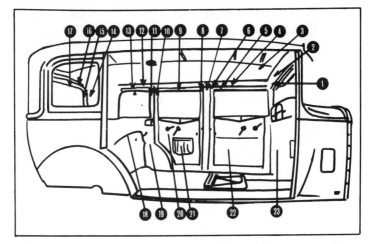

Fig. 7-10. Names of major trim parts in a 1930-style sedan. 1) Windshield regulator board trim. 2) Over windshield trim strip assembly. 3) Headlining with listings attached. 4) Over door weather strip assembly. 5) Front door header trim strip assembly. 6) Front door lock pillar trim strip assembly. 7) Center body pillar trim board assembly. 8) Rear door lock pillar trim strip assembly. 9) Rear door header trim strip assembly. 10) Rear door hinge pillar trim strip assembly. 11) Rear body hinge pillar trim strip assembly. 12) Quarter window header trim strip assembly. 13) Quarter window curtain assembly. 14) Upper quarter trim assembly. 15) Back window glass retainer trim strip assembly. 16) Over back window trim strip assembly. 17) Back window curtain assembly. 18) Rear quarter arm rest assembly. 19) Lower quarter trim assembly. 20) Rear door trim pad assembly. 21) Rear door pocket assembly. 22) Front door trim pad assembly. 23) Cowl trim pad assembly.

surface. The wire or chain is hooked to the tool, and is drawn through the assembly to the surface. Holding tension on the wire or chain, the button is attached, and released, drawing tight against the spring tension (Fig. 7-9).

CURTAINS

During the period of time between the advent of the sedan-type closed car in the 1920s as a best-selling body style and the close of the pre-World War Two era, many cars had pull-down curtains for rear quarter windows and the back window opening (Fig. 7-10). These are often missing, or at least broken, on an unrestored sedan. They are sometimes ignored, the brackets removed and the boarded trim installed without their replacement. They should be replaced if original equipment; not only do curtains give a car a nice, old-timey touch, but they lend an aura of authenticity. Some curtains had fringe along their lower edge, but many did not.

Making new curtains from scratch is possible although it helps, of course, if at least the old roller assembly is still present. To make a set of curtains for, say, a 1931 Chevrolet Sport Sedan you would proceed as follows: Obtain a tinned or chromed metal tube ⅞-inch in diameter. Cut it ¼-inch longer than the finished length will be. Notch the ends so that two ⅛ tabs remain. These tabs should be sized to fit into the original curtain roller ends, if they are available. Otherwise make the tube tabs to fit whatever you will be using for ends. The roller end should be oversized enough that the diameter will match or slightly exceed the diameter of the retracted curtain. Some types of home window shade roller ends can be adapted, or you can make your own. Now place your spring assembly into the tube, fastening the roller ends by bending your tabs over to hold. Cement a piece of black cambric (or similar black material) about 3½-inches wide and the length of the roller to the tube.

The actual curtain fabric should be cut 1¼ inches wider than the roller so that you can hem the sides for a nicely finished look. Cut the fabric lengthwise to six inches beyond the point you wish to be the bottom edge of the extended curtain. This allows a "surplus" of one and a half turns of the curtain on the roller and allows for the ¾-inch pocket you'll be making at the lower edge for the curtain stick.

Finish the curtain hem and the lower edge pocket with double-lap seams. Sew the assembly to the cambric. Install the curtain stick and close the ends of its pockets. Fine silk thread matching the curtain's color was originally used to sew them. Original curtains often had a screw eye in each end of the round curtain stick for a cord which served as a guide when the curtain was going up and down. The cords also helped to keep the curtains from flapping when breeze was streaming through the car and the curtains were down.

Curtain tassels were offered in a variety of types and colors, as they still are today by the few suppliers of tassels left. The tassels were installed on some curtains by spreading the curtain fabric with a trim regulator just above the curtain stick pocket, in the center of the assembly. The tassel loop was threaded through in the center of the assembly, width-wise. It was slipped through the opening, taken down and around the curtain stick pocket and then over the tassel before being drawn tight to secure it. Before making final installation in the car, remove wrinkles from the curtain with a hot iron applied over a damp cloth on the fabric.

Lower edge fringe may be installed on your curtains, although many makes did not have fringed curtains originally.

Chapter 8
Carpeting

Before you buy material and start laying carpet, research in depth what sort of carpet was used originally and determine how it was fastened down.

Very early open cars had floor plates that attached by screws to the wooden floor boards. When closed cars came into favor, carpets got a big boost. For many years most cars had a floor mat of rubber in the front compartment and a rug in the rear. This was in the days when the back seat was the widest, most comfortable seat in the car and the rear seat passenger had the most foot room. He or she had the carpet. It was all a hangover from the days when everyone who was anyone had a chauffer (Fig. 8-1).

Carpets are easily made for most pre-1930s cars since transmission tunnels were all but flat and the body rode on top of the frame instead of around it. As bodies came down to earth, the tunnels got higher. Special care is needed in fitting carpet to the front section of a transmission tunnel. Tunnels not only make a big bump but they often have a flair, too.

On older cars fasteners were used to hold the carpets. The carpets could be removed easily for drying and cleaning. Later, around 1940, the carpet was usually glued to a pad which was in turn cemented to the sheet metal floor (Fig. 8-2). This was harder to take up, of course! The next advance was the elimination of bindings on the edges by hiding the rough edges under door sill plates. Most 1955 and newer cars have rugs secured in this manner (Fig. 8-3).

The original carpet, if present at all, is often too ruined to use for a pattern. But it can give you an idea of where the splits were made for the transmission tunnel when dealing with a front compartment carpet.

MAKING A PATTERN

To make a pattern, remove the front seat assembly and rear seat or whatever is necessary to clear the floor. Use heavy Kraft paper to make a

Fig. 8-1. Carpets were confined to rear compartments of closed cars for many years, except on special models. 1928 Elgin's windows could be removed to give touring car aura. Even at this early date, carpeted kick pads are installed on door trim panel.

pattern, first pushing it down into corners, then tracing around outer edges with a pencil. On carpets with bound edges, allow about ¼-inch of space on the edge of the pattern for sewing the binding on.

Cut the paper out for seat anchorages then paste the paper onto cardboard and trim it for the pattern. If the carpet fastens under sill plates, be sure to leave enough overhang. But if it doesn't and is trimmed with bindings, then don't forget to pull in ¼-inch for the binding.

To cut the carpet, center the pattern on the material, using tailor's chalk to mark the outline. With a sharp knife, cut out the carpet to size.

BINDINGS AND FASTENERS

Binding is normally the same color as the carpet and is made from leatherette strip cut on a bias with a single lap (fold) on each side through which it is stitched to the carpet. Sport jobs often used black binding for light carpets or occasionally matched the color of the upholstery leather. Carpet bindings are strong and require a very heavy-duty sewing machine. The same sort of machine is needed that your leather trim or canvas top requires. Your friend at the awning company might help out here.

Cars with carpets held by fasteners often used a still available Standard-Carr three-prong fastener. This consists of a ring with sharp teeth which are forced through the carpet's backing and cinched down from above. The nap of the carpet hides the teeth. The ring snaps into a base that is screwed into wood floor boards.

Cemented carpets are removed by prying with a putty knife. The insulating material usually comes up, too. These carpets were mostly mohair-type and were used in rear compartments only.

FRONT MAT DIFFICULTIES

Original front floor mats had a variety of patterns. You can probably get a replacement from a mail-order house but it almost certainly will have the wrong pattern. Too, many cars had beige or reddish brown mats. Most replacements are black. Original mats for pre-World War Two cars are scarce and very expensive. Usually dealers in new old stock (never used, but factory produced) advertise original mats "for best offer." To date, no one has reproduced them exactly for any cars but they will no doubt appear someday. Until then a treatment with a polymer rubber solution may help the mat survive.

Fig. 8-2. Carpet for rear floor of 1946 Nash 600 could be easily duplicated. Not so easy is the front mat with carpet inserts. Seats and doors had embossed leatherette kick panels.

75

Fig. 8-3. 1954 Pontiac had full carpeting, used two sections. Edges are trimmed with carpet binding, later were run under sill plates. Vinyl scuff pad below brake pedal minimized wear.

For carpeted front compartments with floor shift levers, start installing the carpet by slipping it over the lever through a pre-cut hole, located by the pattern. For brake, clutch and throttle arms, slit the carpet down from the upper edge to the spot marked for the hole to allow their travel, then open the hole. Keep the holes small but not so much so that the carpet rubs on the pedal in the course of its travel. Many cars had rubber grommets installed around the pedal rods for a weather seal. Replace these grommets if you can find suitable reproductions.

To position fasteners on older cars, first install the bases at the right spots in the floor board. Then rub chalk on the tops of the bases. Position the carpet in place and feel for the bases with your finger, pushing on them to mark the bottom of the carpet. This will show you where to install the rings.

Cars with sunken rear floors present a problem in conforming the carpet to their contours. The remedy is to slit the edge of the carpet, relieving the fullness. The carpet is resewn on the underside when fitted.

Many cars with front compartment carpeting had a rubber heel pad sewn into the carpet on the flat part of the floor right below the pedals. This minimizes wear on the carpets from the pivoting action of heels. These are simply sewn onto carpets.

Reproduction rubber pads for brake, clutch and throttle pedals are available for most popular collector cars. There are still many after-market replacements available, too. A new set of pedals does a lot for a car interior. Rare pedals with monograms or emblems can be custom made but the price is high—as much as $200 a pair!

Chapter 9
Woodgraining

Woodgraining is the application of a realistic woodgrain effect to a metal or other non-wood surface. Most manufacturers used woodgraining from the early 1930s through 1942. Some, notably Chrysler, continued to woodgrain interior metal trim right into the 1950s (Fig. 9-1). The woodgrained instruments and door and window garnishes of pre-war cars were truly beautiful but, sadly, they didn't hold up well. The sun seemed to evaporate the finish off some car dashes.

For many years woodgraining was all but ignored in restoration. It was quite acceptable to paint the dash a nice color. Recently, the trend has been back to the beautiful and authentic woodgraining patterns. A well-grained interior adds a considerable amount to any car's value.

Rich, deep tones of finished wood on an instrument panel have always been a mark of luxury. But the costs of using real, high quality wood made imitation necessary early in the game of mass-produced automobiles.

Woodgraining on metal was used almost from the inception of the automobile. Until 1938, it was usually applied by screen processing. A base color was painted on, then the grain pattern was screened over it (Fig. 9-2).

You can tell if your car has screened woodgrain by taking a close look at the grain. Watch for a fine crosshatch pattern in the contrasting grain color. Often this is most visible near edges that have been covered by other panels or instrument bezels. A screen processor can probably restore these panels, especially if they are flat sections. To exactly reproduce a flat woodgrain, if there is enough of the original left to determine the pattern, have a blow-up photo made on non-glossy paper. Then retouch the grain. The screen processor can reduce the photo down to size and make a screen from it. The screen processor can reproduce

Fig. 9-1. 1941 Chrysler Crown Imperial had burled woodgrain on doors, different pattern on dash. Cowl kick panels were fully carpeted. This was one of first cars to have power windows.

small decals like the one in the glove compartment listing tire pressures and such, too. You can use the enlargement trick to retouch these, too.

THE DI NOC SECRET

During the late 1930s instrument panels became more complex, with curves, depressions and bends stamped into the panel. A new method of wood-graining, called Di Noc, was developed about this time. Di Noc used actual photographs of woodgrain to get the pattern on a clear backing that dissolved into a base coat when applied. Detroit applied the Di Noc to flat sheet metal, then stamped their instrument panels into shape. This was their great secret.

Di Noc was acquired by the 3-M Company and it swept the industry. 3-M greatly improved Di Noc's staying power under the sun's light but not until it was largely lost on instrument panels.

Today, Di Noc is still very much alive. It is used on sporty station wagons to give that traditional air of country elegance. It reappears on interior metal trim from time to time although plastic wood is the current rage. All kinds of appliances are adorned in Di Noc.

Di Noc is still made by 3-M in a wide array of patterns. You can use it in your restoration, if you can find a source of supply. 3-M won't help you much. They "do not retain inventories of old patterns," according to a spokesperson, nor are they interested in you as a small purchaser of a few yards of their material. Your area 3-M branch's Decorative Products Division might be able to get you a sample roll of 100 square feet of a given current pattern for around $80, so if you can locate a suitable grain and identify it, and can work up a shared order with some others, you might be

Fig. 9-2. Even Model A Ford DeLuxe models used woodgrain on dash trim panel and door garnish moldings.

able to deal direct. Cruising late model used car lots in search of Di Noc appliques on recent station wagons might help you find a grain—ask the original dealer if he has any Di Noc grained film in stock, he might have a nice remainder lying around from a repair job (Fig. 9-3).

Fig. 9-3. The 1940 Oldsmobile 98 interior boasted the most intricate woodgrain patterns ever used. It was a Di Noc grain, applied to the flat panel, which was afterwards stamped to shape. The plastic wheel, beautiful when new, soon cracked and warped.

Di Noc is not confined to woodgrain patterns. Many early 1950s cars used Di Noc transfers to approximate engine-turned dash and door panels. Other metallic-type patterns were and are used. Perhaps you are certain that you cannot find a Di Noc to match your car's woodgraining. Or, maybe the thought of working flat sheets of Di Noc onto your contoured and rounded instrument panel makes you weak in the knees. Don't give up on woodgraining—there is yet another method of woodgrain restoration.

Before we get to that, however, we'll take a look at modern and not-so-modern Di Noc applications, and cover the preparations for any woodgraining job.

PREPARE FOR GRAINING

No matter which method of woodgraining you choose, it will work best if you remove the panel or molding to be grained from your car. Once you have effected the removal, strip the part to be grained down to bare metal. On an instrument panel you will want to remove all gauges, knobs, trim strips and such. You will be amazed at the myriad wires, cables and other things clinging to the back of the panel (the newer the car, the worse it will be). Take proper precautions by labeling wires and other parts so you'll know where they go when it all comes together again some day, weeks or months hence. You might even make a schematic diagram for yourself and/or use your camera to record the scene before total disassembly begins.

Once the sheet metal is stripped of parts it must be stripped of the old finish. Before you do this, though, make sure you have identified the original color and grain used on the metal. Background colors are usually related to brown, running from warms tans to earthy dark tones and even almost-oranges. Some cars had a grey cast to their background or "base" color. You'll want to have a base color matched and mixed if you are using transluscent Di Noc or are going to hand grain the panel. You can often find traces of the original grain pattern and under color on surfaces that were covered, such as behind the glove box door, under nameplates and behind emblems and trim strips.

On many cars the dash and window reveals may have been painted by a used car dealer or owner to cover sun-faded grain. This sort of damage was usually on the horizontal surfaces, while the more vertical, shaded areas may have been good yet. Sand gently down through the coats of paint and expose the original pattern.

Here again, your camera can record the grain pattern for future reference. If no trace of original grain can be salvaged, refer to your original sales literature and club publications. Don't forget your camera when you attend any car show—just in case an intact original presents itself for inspection (Fig. 9-4).

PREPARING THE PANEL

Now that you have the color and grain accurately recorded, strip the old paint, pinstripes, flames, original Di Noc and whatever else from the

Fig. 9-4. Woodgrained metal imitated genuine wood trim such as used on the custom-built Lincoln Willoughby Sport Sedan.

panel. Paint remover will do, but many restorers prefer a chemical hot tank dip, since this will also take care of the reverse side of the panel and clean out the crimped edges around the panel. If any rust remains it should be removed by sanding or even hitting the panel with light sandblasting.

Many older cars have a habit of acquiring extra holes in their instrument panels where extra after-market accessories were mounted. Fix them now, filling dents and depressions at the same time with regular auto body repair materials. Get a smooth surface, but remember, you can use epoxy and other filler since you won't be plating this surface.

TWO TYPES OF DI NOC

A big change was made in the Di Noc line for 1967. After years of being applied by a solvent and adhesive process, Di Noc got a backing and became a pressure-sensitive product. You may still be able to locate the earlier type, however. It is more forgiving and easier to work with than the new stuff. It is also much messier.

Applying Di Noc (Early Type)

You'll need bonding adhesive for the old style Di Noc. Try a local car dealer who carries a line that featured "woodie" wagons in the 1950s and 1960s. You may be able to get a pint from him. Satisfy yourself once again that the panel you are going to grain is clean and absolutely smooth, then spray on the bonding adhesive with a small spray gun, or if no other way

81

can be found, with a universal aerosol bomb. Spray just enough to cover the surface. The sprayed adhesive will take about half an hour to set. It is ready when you can touch with your finger and not leave a print. (Touch an area that will be covered, in case you *do* leave a print.)

While the adhesive is setting up, make a rough pattern on your sheet of Di Noc for installation. Leave plenty of overhang to pull on while working the material. Usually, cover right over the glove box door and cut it out later. On some cars there will be a chrome molding splitting the dash panel. If so, take advantage of the situation and do a half panel at a time, for the smaller the section you are working, the easier the Di Noc will be to handle.

To remove the Di Noc from its backing immerse it in water, just like the flame decals you used to plaster all over plastic model cars as a kid. When it is nearly ready for removal spray a strip of the instrument panel with a solvent solution called M-E-K. This is available from your local car dealer, too, with some luck. It dissolves the adhesive and the nitrocellulose bottom layer of the Di Noc, bonding them together. The woodgrain itself is vinyl and is not affected.

Slide the Di Noc off its paper backing and onto the section with M-E-K, working from the center out. Use your thumb or something suitable and clean to work out bubbles. Even dust grains will cause bumps so keep everything wiped down.

Di Noc gives you about 15 minutes to play with before it gets really sticky. Get a good bite on the first part before spraying more M-E-K on and moving out. To stretch it into depressions and around corners and rolls heat the Di Noc with a heat lamp behind the panel. This makes it quite flexible. After covering the side of the panel with the glove box door, cut out the door opening and wrap the rough edges over the lip of the door.

Applying Pressure-Sensitive Di Noc

New type Di Noc can be used equally well. You may *have* to use it, in fact, since the old Di Noc is getting rather hard to find. The new type just peels off and sticks on. But you can make it adjustable by covering the panel with a regular dishwashing detergent. This keeps the adhesive from being activated before you want it to be making a film between it and the panel.

A roller squeegee is supplied by 3-M to car dealers for rolling out the soap and bubbles. You may be able to buy one or to adapt a suitable roller. This Di Noc can be heated to increase its give and flexibility, too. Stretch it first, then roll out the detergent. Modern Di Noc is very durable and won't peel.

WOODGRAINING BY HAND

The other method of woodgraining mentioned involves the application of the grain pattern with your own hand. Your sense of creativity is heightened with this opportunity to display your artistic flair, as you create beautiful grains closely duplicating the original woodgrain pattern used on your car. Woodgraining by hand is especially practical (as opposed to pressure-sensitive transfers) for window garnishes made in one stamped piece to surround a window opening. Many of these were originally grained either by a printing process or with a roller operation. You could not get the pressure-sensitive transfer all over the molding in one piece, and even doing it with seams is fraught with difficulty and generates an expensive pile of wasted material.

Hand woodgraining begins with the same steps as those used to start a pressure-sensitive application. The instrument panel and other pieces to be grained should be removed from the vehicle, stripped and prepared for the application of a primer and base color. Be careful when sanding down to reveal the original grain, since some grains had a cross-grain effect that might be sanded off before you realize what it is. Original sales literature or an original car should be consulted before sanding.

There are several different methods of woodgraining by hand. Some restorers use acrylic automotive lacquer. Others use a lacquer base from hardware store antique woodgrain kits. Many pros prefer nitrocellulose automotive lacquer, which is no longer made and is hard to obtain. The acrylic lacquers are automotive exterior finishes, so you might find just the right shade on your neighbor's new sedan or by a trip to local car lots.

Whichever base coat is chosen, select a color as close to the original as possible. Spray the panel with a compatible primer after reinstalling the glove box door, ashtrays that are grained and any other parts that are part of the flowing surface of the grain pattern. This is important—your work will flow across the parts and they must be together when you begin.

The base paint is ideally applied with a compressor-driven spray gun over the primer, which has been sanded with #400 wet-dry paper. Acrylic lacquer should be thinned to a 3:1 ratio. You can use a similar mixture with a universal spray bomb if a compressor cannot be pressed into service. Successful base coats have even been applied with spray cans and some adventurous souls even mix the paint right on the panel, a touchy method at best.

Don't polish or rub out the base coat. The graining needs a slightly roughened surface to adhere to. Lightly sand with wet #400 sandpaper to remove excessive roughness.

APPLYING GRAINING PAINT

Graining paint is available from any store selling antiquing kits. Some restorers prefer to use a rubber base printer's ink, which is obtainable from print shop suppliers. Experiment with the ink to see if it suits your needs. There are many ways of applying the grain. Professional wood-graining brushes are available, but costly. At the other end of the scale is the common household rag. This is a very crude woodgraining tool and should be avoided, but you will see some examples of graining obviously turned out with this equipment at most car shows.

How you apply the grain will determine the ultimate effect. Using a bit of imagination you can do beautiful graining without expending cash for tools. Sponges, cheese cloth, the edge of a stiff bird feather, even a crumpled newspaper page can be effective. A graining "comb" can be fashioned by bending the teeth of a cheap plastic comb to make uneven spaces; or you can buy genuine professional graining combs. Bob Dunham, a California graining expert showed *Skinned Knuckles* how he makes his beautiful soft burl patterns. He puts on his ink-solvent solution rather heavily, then blows on the wet solution with a soda straw. The results are spectacular. Dunham prefers to use rubber-base printers ink for his woodgraining. He says he spent many hours finding the right blend of ink and solvent for graining, but once he found it it has been very reliable. One advantage of the ink is that it stays wet and on top of the base coat until the finish coat of nitrocellulose clear lacquer (he doesn't use acrylic clear lacquer for a finish coat—says it is prone to give an off-color effect) seals it. The clear lacquer Dunham uses is made by Ditzler for engine applications. Therefore, he can easily wipe off areas that are not satisfactory or that have been disturbed. Others use enamel retarder with regular graining paint. It increases the flow and blurs the definition between graining paint and base paint, since it sinks the graining color right into the base. If you use too much enamel retarder the patterns may become too indistinct. Here, there is no second chance, either. It is an art form so develop a feel for it.

Practice graining using a sponge at first to make the knot holes and duplicate burl patterns so popular on garnish moldings (Fig. 9-5). Using the rough edge of the sponge, draw it across the panel in a constant wavy motion to make a flowing grain. Always keep in mind that the work should flow. Approximate the locations for knotholes and other pattern deviations. You can't stop and line them up exactly. Don't worry. Even the pedantic legions in the hobby will not notice a knot hole that is half an inch out of place.

Woodgraining is more an effect than an absolute. Your work will be judged on overall flow and integral conformity.

LITTLE THINGS MATTER

You can wipe out any section with a wet cloth or paper towel before the graining paint dries.

Some panels were grained twice with an overgrain running across the main grain. To apply overgrain, use a coat of Varathane on acrylic lacquer, then apply the overgrain. Be very cautious.

Crosswise streaking can be softened by sanding the surface with #600 grit sandpaper. Another coat of Varathane will help control the blending. Thin graining paint for this job with clear enamel and use a graining comb or your own tool for applying the cross grain.

A flat fitch brush is best for woodgraining and is obtainable from any art store. The brush can be modified for graining by notching the bristles. A blending brush or clean rag can be used to blend graining paint.

Fig. 9-5. Even Nash's line-leading 600 had a beautifully woodgrained dash with engine turned face panels and plastic radio speaker grille, all of which means hours of restoration work.

To create a porous textured look the completed base and primary grain should be coated with Varathane, then sprinkled with graining paint. To do this, flick the brush across a hair comb, making the specks fly. Brush blender across the specks to give the pore effect.

Water-base acrylic wood stains are also suitable for graining and are applied similarly to lacquers. Since they are water soluble, they have certain disadvantages and advantages. The main disadvantage is that the work must be thoroughly sealed after the graining is finished since water would wash away what was exposed. The pulses included easy erasure— just rinse off the part you don't like. Brushes and yourself are quite washable, too. And the product is odorless. The water-base stains dry to a very smooth finish.

Woodgraining by hand is tedious and not for the uncreative. It requires, and stimulates, individual experimentation. A successful job is a very real accomplishment and every time you confront those smooth, flowing and beautifully tranquil grain lines on the instrument panel, you'll know it was worth the effort. A nice woodgrain job impresses everyone from judges to aunts. If you enjoy the work and are good at it, you'll get plenty of chances to practice the art when work gets around about your talent.

Chapter 10
The Big Headache—Plastic

It was love at first sight. Auto makers discovered plastic in the early 1930s and immediately set about adapting it to automobile interiors, using it for knobs, escutcheons and other adornments (Fig. 10-1). Most companies (except Ford) used a cellulose base plastic. Unlike the old Bakelite, used for many years for horn buttons, the new plastics were not dull; they had a beautiful and mysterious translucent glow to them when new. Ford used a soybean plastic. It took a nice finish but lacked the translucent quality of the cellulose stuff.

Plastic reached the height of its popularity, at least as far as collector cars are concerned, in 1940. By the time World War II was over, many disgruntled car owners were complaining because plastic turned out to be just what it cracked up to be. That was because heat caused shrinkage and warpage. In extreme cases the plastic would melt right out of its bezels. Steering wheels cracked so badly they looked like half the plastic had fallen off. Ashtrays would bend nearly double. Even Ford's soybean derivative quickly developed age wrinkles and warped like a funhouse mirror (Fig. 10-2).

Car buyers didn't like the cracking and warping one bit so plastic went on vacation in most cars for a few years after the war. Still, the allure of its cheapness and adaptability to built-in coloring couldn't be denied. When plastic came back in the mid-1950s it was much more durable. This time it came to stay.

The very cars that used the troublesome early plastics are currently among the most popular collector cars. Replacing this plastic is one of the restorer's biggest headaches. Many of the pieces are small but they are important trim details and no car looks complete without them.

Fig. 10-1. Cadillac used plastic on 1938 60-S center instrument grille. Owner of this car traded a running Cadillac engine for reproduced plastic assembly.

SURVIVORS UNLIKELY

Don't waste time looking for good plastic in junkyard cars. The cars have been outside so long that the plastic will probably have crumbled to dust. Dealers usually ran out of replacements long ago so don't expect miracles there, either. Today, there is an incredible demand for mint plastic parts for late 1930s and early 1940s cars. A perfect original steering wheel for a 1941 Cadillac costs more than a whole parts car. If you don't want it, there will be dozens of restorers standing in line behind you. One of them will be willing to pay the price.

The demand for plastic trim has become so great that some vendors within the hobby have started supplying reproduction plastic for popular cars like pre-war Ford V-8s. These Ford parts are widely advertised in hobby publications by large commercial firms. Reproduction parts for other popular cars, such as pre-war Buicks, are often made by part-time hobbyists who have learned the art of plastic reproduction and are engaged in a service to the fellow hobbyists by continuing to reproduce badly needed and impossible to find plastic trim items. These fellows, who often charge a very reasonable price, advertise heavily in club publications where their message goes right to the customer—another reason why joining a club is important.

Steering wheels can be rebuilt. You can use a hard filler, like the plastic used to fill body dents, to build up between the cracks. The plastic was molded to a metal ring, so there shouldn't be a warpage problem. Sand the filler as close to the original contour as you can. Painting with heavy coats of enamel gives a finished look, although it will lack the translucence of the original.

At least one commercial business specializes in steering wheel repair. They dip the wheel in liquified DuPont Tenite solution. This is the same process that gives a hard shiny finish to bowling balls. Tenite butylate crystals are used to give the color. The major problem in this process is getting a uniform depth and working the finger grip contours on the back edge of the wheel into their proper shape and spacing.

MAKING YOUR OWN

You can reproduce small plastic parts yourself and the process might even be useful for reproducing larger items like steering wheels. We'll examine two popular methods of reproduction later.

Quality is important in the materials used as is their compatibility with other products. When using casting resin to reproduce a knob, it is recommended that you use G.E. silicone rubber #630 and a clear casting resin such as sold by Sears stores for casting components. The rubber for the mold can be purchased from a chemical company for about $10 a pound. The resin runs $5-$7 a gallon.

Before you begin, you'll need a usable sample of the part you want to duplicate. A good place to find this might be through a local club chapter. Look very confident when asking another club member to let you use his knob because he probably won't be too thrilled with the idea. The process isn't dangerous for the knob, rest assured, but be sure to treat it as the treasure it is and don't lose or drop it.

MAKING A KNOB

Making a typical knob begins with a simple paper tube, slightly larger than the knob you are reproducing. It should be about ¼-inch higher and ½-inch wider. Close off one end with masking tape.

Clean the knob thoroughly, removing small scratches and burrs. Smooth the surface with a fine rubbing compound. Toothpaste works surprisingly well. The smoother the pattern knob, the less hand finishing the reproductions will require.

If the knob is a gearshift knob or something similar with a metal insert for threads, you will have to make up an insert from brass tapped tubing. Or, reclaim an insert from your old knob or a salvage knob. The plastic itself may have been threaded on some cars. This can be accomplished on your reproduction with some forethought.

To make a mold, apply a general purpose wax to the pattern knob and insert it into the molding tube, pushing the flat end against the sticky surface of the masking tape across the bottom. Center the knob in the tube.

Next, mix the molding materials. Follow directions on the containers in mixing R.T.V. rubber. Make enough to fill the mold container. Be very precise in mixing, as you should always be when mixing chemicals that rely on self-generating heat to cure. Roy Tucker, whose article in the Lincoln-Zephyr Owners Club magazine inspired this chapter, suggests fresh, non-waxed paper cups for mixing. They are readily disposable, of course. Never re-use your mixing containers since the residue will contaminate other mixtures.

Fig. 10-2. Ford's 1940 Standard models used plastic knobs, steering wheel, door handle escutcheons. Steering wheel held up well but knobs often disintegrate with time. Round knobs can be reproduced on lathe or by mold.

When the rubber and hardener are ready, pour them into the mold, tapping the edges of the mold to help the mixture settle. Make sure it is full to the brim when finished. Let the mixture cure overnight. Then, peel off the paper tube. You'll see the bottom of the knob where it was stuck to the tape.

Work the knob around in the mold until it is loose, then gently work it out of the mold. If the part is not shaped so it can be easily removed, you may cut an opening down one side with a razor blade and remove the pattern piece. Close the slit with a straight pin through the mold at a 90-degree angle to the cut, carefully aligning the walls. Wrap the mold with masking tape to insure a good seal.

USING THE MOLD

Once you have a successful mold, proceed with making a new knob. While mixing resin, pay close attention to mixing directions. Buy resin color at the store where you obtained the resin. It is mixed in the resin before the hardener is added. Be very careful to get just the right shade of color. The resins give that very desirable translucent quality, closely approximating original plastic. For Fords and Lincolns, use oil coloring base pigments (available in tubes) to give an authentic, solid opaque look which polishes to a deep luster. The pigments are much more suitable to color matching since they are available in infinite varieties. You can also use fiberglass resin coloring, as used in boat repairing.

Mix color to satisfaction in a non-waxed cup or other container. Then, pour in the hardener and pour the mixture into the mold. Slightly overfill for settling but don't overfill so much that the mixture overflows. Tap the mold a bit.

The resin mixture will cure in less than an hour at room temperature. If your knob needs a tapped insert, here is where you take care of it. Roy Tucker says to fill the mold about half full, then thread a soft wood dowel into the stud and fit it into the mold, resting the insert on the bottom of the mold. Push a straight pin through the soft dowel so it will just rest on the lip of the mold. This keeps the stud flush and lets you center it (Fig. 10-3).

Finish pouring the resin. You won't need a parting agent or mold releaser. R.T.V. rubber usually won't adhere to casting resins. When the resin has cured, work the new knob out just as you did the original when making the mold. You should have a near perfect replica. Smooth off flash with a jeweler's file or 400 wet-dry sandpaper. Polish the knob with a white polishing compound. Paint in dots or letters as needed and install the sparkling new knob on your car. Keep the mold and materials. You'll have plenty of use for them when fellow enthusiasts get word you're making knobs.

MACHINING A KNOB

The second way to make a new knobs is by machining. This time you buy a rod of nylon or similar synthetic material. Look for a supplier in the yellow pages under plastics, rods, tubes, and sheets. Take a sample of the knob you wish to reproduce and show the salesman what you have in mind.

Nylon is porous, which means it will take a dye. Even good old household RIT dye will work on nylon. To get a gloss finish, spray the finished knob with clear lacquer.

You'll need a pattern knob, of course, and a lathe to get started. Even a small wood lathe will do. Then, you make a template or former out of metal, unless you have a very simple knob and a very steady hand.

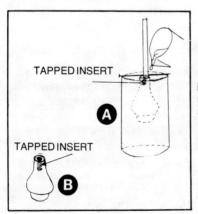

TAPPED INSERT

A

TAPPED INSERT

B

Fig. 10-3. To install tapped metal insert in reproduction plastic knob made by mold process, thread onto soft dowel, using straight pin to align and hold flush with edge of mold, as shown in A. Finished reproduction know with insert in phantom view, B.

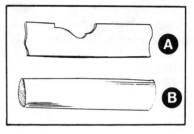

Fig. 10-4. Starting with original knob, forming tool (A) is made by machine shop. Nylon tube (B) is turned down on lathe, using forming tool to check shape. Reproduction knob is result. Grooves around knob are easily cut. Letters are put on with engraver's pantograph.

The former is ground out of a blank "cut-off tool" obtainable from any machine shop supply house. The section of ¼-inch thick steel for the former should cost you under $5.

Using the pattern knob to check, grind the silhouette of the knob into the former. Don't forget, the steel gets hot when being ground. Quench it with water before fitting the knob to it, each time.

Grooves in the knob are cut later. Use a handstone or other finisher to round out your former and smooth it. The form tool is ready when you can see just the tiniest glimmer of light uniformly around the knob as it is fitted to the tool.

Chuck the nylon into the lathe and fit the form tool into its holder. You are ready to start cutting the new knob now. While cutting, constantly compare the new knob taking form with the original, thus avoiding mistakes.

Use a cutting tool to put in grooves. Measure and mark the new knob carefully to make sure grooves are correctly spaced and the proper depth. Once you've got the process down pat you can run knobs off to your heart's content.

A machine shop might make the reproduction knobs for you. They could make a tool and runoff a bunch, but they probably would rather be doing something more profitable. The more they make, the cheaper they get, so don't even think about it unless you have a stack of orders to make it practical.

Reproduction brass knobs can also be made with the forming tool and lathe.

Nylon knobs are lettered with a pantograph. Dots and grooves can be painted on before the lacquer is applied.

A milling machine and a competent operator can duplicate virtually any item that has a basically round cross section, so there is hope for even those most complex knobs (Fig. 10-4).

PLATED PLASTICS

By the mid-1950s plastic steering wheels (Fig. 10-5), knobs and handles had become very durable. In fact they seldom need replacing on cars of this era unless they have been harshly abused. Just about the time that all the old plastics problems were seemingly on the road to solution a new set of durability problems developed.

The metallic plating of plastics was a desirable goal for auto manufacturers long before it became an accepted reality. (Some pre-war cars had examples of plating on *glass*, such as the 1937 Buick stop lamp assembly.) Plastic parts could be removed from their mold and plated without the expensive and time-consuming buffing process. They were much lighter than metal parts and they were not susceptible to galvanic corrosion (Fig. 10-6).

The first commercial plating of plastics used a process in which the surface to be plated was roughened to give the metallic coating something to hang on to. The resulting finish was rough and not really any more shiny than sprayed aluminum paint. (An example of this early plating is the promotional model cars of the early 1950s.) Others used a vapor and vacuum method which left a bright but shallow layer of metallic substance on the plastic.

By 1963 an all-chemical process had been developed that made plated plastics a reality in American automobiles. This process chemically altered the surface of the type of plastic used (most often ABS— acrylonitrile-butadiene-styrene) which induced an interchange of the metal and plastic atoms. To quote R.G. Huber, writing in *Skinned Knuckles*, the hobby restoration journal, "At this point plastic plated with metal was a feasible alternative to many all-metal parts. Plated plastic now had the look and feel of metal without the weight, cost and labor of metal parts."

Plating processes for the deposition of metal on other types of plastics followed in quick succession. Some of the early ABS interior parts were very durable and shiny, especially if they were used in an area where

Fig. 10-5. Restored "banjo" wheel on 1938 Cadillac 60-S has original opaque look. Later transluscent wheels are hard to reproduce.

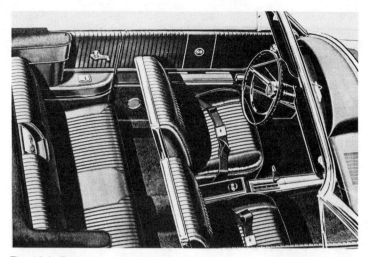

Fig. 10-6. Plated plastics were used increasingly in the 1960's. Arm rest assemblies on 1964 Impala SS are just one application (courtesy Chevrolet).

abrasion was minimal—such as behind an upholstered armrest board. But, the process hasn't held up so well on other types of plastic. Depending on the plated material and the metallic process used, some parts are susceptible to wearing off. Other types resist abrasion but tend to peel with age. The outlining "chrome" on the soft dashboards of the late 1960s and the 1970s is especially fragile; a good auto polish will take it right off with a little pressure.

Replating plastic parts has become a hot topic among restorers of mid-1960s muscle and pony cars. Good used parts are almost impossible to find. Supposedly, a few platers are now offering plastic replating, but they maintain a low profile since they have plenty of business. According to R.G. Huber the process involves a chemically-applied metallic coating on the plastic prior to the more familiar type of electroplating, and the process is within the scope of most plater's capabilities. Unless they are gouged or scratched, plastic parts should be replatable with minimum processing, since they do not pit like metal.

To keep your plastic "chrome" in good shape always avoid using any abrasive compound on it. Use diluted chemical cleaners instead. Even here, be extremely gentle, and once you get it clean keep it that way. Even fine dust is gritty enough to scratch the plastic's plated surface, especially if the plastic is soft to begin with. Reproductions of popular car's plated plastic interior trim items are beginning to appear right now and no doubt many more will follow.

Check the "Services" columns of your hobbyist periodicals for ads offering replating services.

Chapter 11
Convertible Tops

Convertibles, regardless of make, are likely to be the prime collector cars for generations to come. Right now, roadsters and phaetons—convertibles without roll-up glass windows (they have side curtains for weather protection)—are the hottest old cars and convertibles are close behind.

A Wisconsin upholstery shop owner reported he did nearly 75 convertible tops during 1974, far more than he had done in a 12-month period for many years. More and more people are picking up on convertibles as ideal sunny-day second cars with appreciation potential.

Convertibles do have their own unique problems. The older ones were usually outfitted in expensive leather upholstery. Their interiors were often water-soaked, especially during the years they were too worthless to warrant new, good quality tops. As a result, they often have rusted floor pans. The most obvious problem involves fabric or synthetic tops which shrink, tear and deteriorate (Fig. 11-1).

REPLACING A TOP

Replacing a top is possible for the home restorer. Even the big general line mail order houses carry tops for most cars back as far as the mid-1930s. Wholesale suppliers to the upholstery trade can still supply tops for virtually any car and, if they can't, the skilled upholsterer can make patterns and a top himself (Fig. 11-2).

Putting a convertible top on is one thing. Putting it on right is quite another. As in all upholstering, extra care must be given to shaping and alignment.

Before installing the new top, try to determine just what sort of top is authentic for your car. Very rarely does a convertible more than a decade

Fig. 11-1. Virtually every area of interior restoration will be utilized in restoring this convertible's interior and top. Nearly every job can be done by home restorer, though.

or so old have its original top. For authenticating your car, the best source is a car with the original top. If you are fortunate enough to find one, be especially careful to note details of the trim. Write down what sort of tips were used on binding, what color the binding was, where and how many fasteners were used, and what type they are.

While inspecting an original or authenticated restoration, also note the construction and material used to make the top boot. On early cars they were canvas or rubberized fabric, like the tops. Later, vinyl was popular. Some cars, like the mid-1950s Cadillac Eldorados, used fiberglass boots.

Top Framework

Before installing a new top, the framework or bows should be restored. Wood that is rotted should be replaced, and proper chrome or paint work done. Proper alignment of the top's bows and framework is essential to having a close-fitting and smooth top.

If your car has been outside for a long time, just folding the top will be a chore. Don't expect a long-idle electric pump motor and old, weak, hydraulic lines to do the job for you. Better to release pressure in the system by disconnecting the hydraulic lines, catching the fluid in a container instead of having it spray all over the paint work and interior when a hose bursts.

95

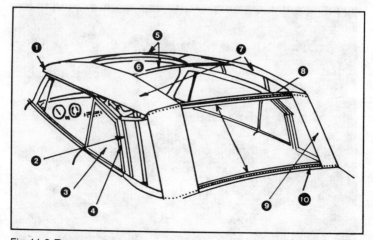

Fig. 11-2. Top parts of a typical pre-1950 convertible with top covering removed: 1) Front bow and tacking strip; 2) Side roof rail; 3) Rear quarter window; 4) Weather strip channel; 5) Center bows; 6) Top pads; 8) Top rear bow; 9) Rear quarter trim pads; 10) Rear trim rail.

Free rusted or stick hinges with a penetrating rust dissolver. Don't hammer on the joints or try to force the top down. The hardest to find and most expensive parts on your car are the top pieces. If you break a link, it may take years to find a replacement and it will probably cost you a goodly amount of cash to obtain it.

Most pre-1940 tops were manually-operated. Then, in 1940, several cars had vacuum-powered tops. The next year, electric motors driving screws were used. Virtually all 1950s tops were hydraulic.

On very old cars, bows are wood. Even later pre-war cars used wood healer bows, and sometimes rear bows. Some top wood is reproduced for popular antiques. The "services" columns of antique publications can help isolate suppliers. On rare models, you'll have to do it yourself or find a good woodworker to do it for you (Fig. 11-3).

Top Sources

Several grades of replacement tops are available from mail order houses. Since the difference in cost isn't that great, order a good quality top. If you want more authenticity, talk to a local auto upholsterer. He might be able to get a good factory-style replacement top from one of his wholesalers.

Another good place to look for tops is the car dealer who sells your make of car. He often installs convertible tops and may have a new one gathering dust in the loft. Sometimes the stock will go back 20 years.

Most 1950 and older convertible tops are canvas or rubberized fabric. During the 1950s, the swing to synthetics began, with vinyl emerging dominant. Tops originally were offered in many colors by car makers. But they are usually black or white when replaced. Blue, tan, and green were popular in the color-conscious 1950s though these colors and more were offered from the mid-1930s on.

INSTALLING A REPLACEMENT

To install a top, begin by removing the top from its shipping box and draping it right over the remnants of the old top to check general fit. If the top has original-type, stitched seams instead of more modern heat-sealed seams, waterproof the stiches. Do this on a clean floor or table before installing the top. Gently open the inner flap of the seam and apply a good sealant with a small pressure gun or similar device. Keep the sealant handy as we will use it again it on the rear trim sticks on some cars and on the seam above the rear bow on all of them.

Right around 1954 most car makers changed the method of tacking convertible tops around the rear and quarter sections. Old-style tops have the boot studs (to which the boot snaps fasten) right through the lower trim binding or rail. Newer cars with the modern method have these studs in a chrome trim molding around the lower edge of the top (Fig. 11-4).

On the early convertibles, start removing the old top by taking out the boot studs. Mark their location by making a chalk line on the sheet metal of the car body. Next, move to the side windows and, with the top partially raised, remove the rear window weather strips on each side. On older cars the rubber part of the strip usually slips out of the metal retainer, exposing the screws that hold it on. Newer cars may have studs with nuts holding the weather strips on. Carefully remove them. The weather strip assemblies may be adjustable. If they were sealing okay, mark their position. If they were out of alignment, make sure to adjust them when re-installing.

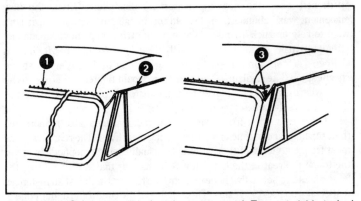

Fig. 11-3. 1) Older convertible front bows are wood. Top material is tacked above previously installed single-cord welt; 2) Binding edge; 3) After top front edge is tacked and trimmed; V-shaped flap is cut out and resulting length of binding edge is pulled around corner of top and tacked.

Fig. 11-4. Top covering is loosened by removing inside trim sticks on post-1954 style convertibles. Rolled-up, it reveals rear quarter stay pads.

Aligning Touring Bows

Many touring cars are restored with the top bows incorrectly positioned when the new top material is installed. Often, the bow placement was retained from the old top installation, and again, it isn't wise to rely on such a guide. "The old time trim shops never made any attempt to make it like it was originally," says Jim Willems of McPherson College's restoration school. "They were trying to do the quickest and cheapest job," he explains. The trimmers would tighten the bows to the point where slack was removed from the material, paying no attention to the finished silhouette of the car.

Other cars suffer from owner or trimmer's attempts to "modernize" their top lines at one time or another during their lives. The rear bow is the most frequent victim of these attempts, usually being "chopped" to lower the top at the rear of the body. Jim Willems says that in fitting a top, the bows should be set so that none of them lean forward in almost all instances (especially on pre-1933 cars). The belt line of the car (or the upper edge of the doors and body from the cowl back) was usually parallel to the lower part of the top on touring cars. A shortened rear bow will cause this parallel line of the top material to sag from the rear bow ahead to the next bow forward—a frequently seen but almost never correct posture for an erected top.

"Even if you are off only an inch on a car like a Model T Ford touring car, it will make it look funny even to the slightly experienced eye," Willems warns.

Bows are "numbered" from front to rear in trimming and most touring cars have four bows. Any misalignment will affect all but the #1 bow in most cases.

Taking measurements on a car that is proven "right" can help position bows, and photos of such a car can be invaluable aids, especially if they are full side views. Many times the correct positioning of bows is found by trial and error fitting and a sense of proper esthetic proportions (Fig. 11-5).

When There Is No Guide

"It is unrealistic to believe you'll get the original top on your forty or fifty year old car," Jim Willems tells his students at McPherson College. Even if the top appears to be quite old it has probably been replaced and is incorrect. "Most trim shops threw away what was hard to do and did it in their own patterns when replacing tops," Willems cautions.

Back windows, in particular, are likely to be incorrect replacements on older cars. Many times a new top had a simple, single panel plastic-type rear window sewn into the back curtain in place of the original (perhaps cracked) beveled glass and oval metal frame. Other cars may have simple oval or rectangular frames in place of the four or five small and elegant diamond-shaped isinglass windows formerly sewn into the curtain.

"You can go to 20 different restorations and find 20 different types of top installations or methods. In most cases they probably faithfully reproduced what was on it, but that may not have been right," says Jim Willems. Usually when a trimmer replaced a top he eliminated half or more

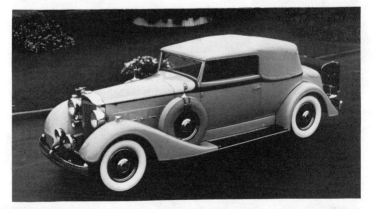

Fig. 11-5. The kind of fit that is required to produce trophies is illustrated by top installation on the R.E. Milhous Packard, one of the top showcars in the West (courtesy John C. Meyer III.)

of the little leather straps and buckles originally installed on the top (Fig. 11-6). Cars with original tops are almost impossible to find, as are detailed photos of top assemblies for elderly cars. This will call for extra detective work. Perhaps a very complete full-line catalog can be found showing details of the top, or even an advertisement emphasizing the top will help.

You can determine if your car's top is original by lifting the material along a nailed strip and inspecting the nail holes. The tack strips will have more holes than nails if the top has been replaced, since tacks are always driven in random placement and land in old holes coincidentally and infrequently. If your car definitely has the original top, go over it *very* carefully before discarding it. Make notes and take photos of details such as type of stitch used, location and type of buckles and straps, type of rear window, and such. You might be able to salvage and re-use many of the fasteners. In fact, you might wish to store the old top away in a box for future reference even if it is so gross that you wish to discard it right away. You might settle some interesting judging disputes with the old material someday.

REMOVAL DETAILS

To remove the old-style top, take out the screws or tacks holding the quarter flaps. These are usually exposed by removal of the weather strips. Untack the top around the car trim rail. Also, untack from the necessary bows, removing the front bow weather strip if necessary, and remove the top.

On newer convertibles, the lower edges of the top are tacked to removable tacking strips hidden by the well that the top folds into. Detach the well material at the seat back, then feel for the screws or bolts holding it at the rear and remove it.

You will see the trim sticks as soon as the well is out. There will be three of them, usually, and they are attached with screws. Remove them and untack the top material from them. Then open the wire-on binding on the rear bow and untack this strip. Put the metal finishing tips from the binding in a safe place. They are not easy to replace. The rear curtain, which houses the rear window, will be loose on the lower edge already. You can now remove it when it is loosened at the bow. Quarter stay pads, the padded strips running from the outer ends of the bow to the trim stick, can also be removed for repair or replacement.

Most 1950s and newer tops have flaps built into them that are cemented at the rear-quarter windows and just above the front vent windows. Loosen these.

Carefully remove the header bow weather strip. It is an important part of the top's weather sealing. Under the strip (above it, actually) are the tacks holding the top fabric at the front. Remove these. Most early convertibles had snaps built into the edges to keep the sides from drawing up (Fig. 11-7). For a few years during the 1950s it was thought the new materials being used wouldn't need such devices so tops in these years do

Fig. 11-6. Replacing a top includes all the little details, such as the top hold-down strap on 1927 Model T Ford touring.

not have any provision to hold the edges above the side windows. The synthetics pulled up just as badly as ever so by the mid-1960s a new method had been devised. This method uses a tension wire through a lengthwise pocket on each edge of the top. The wires are removable. Just undo them at both ends and take them out after the top is off.

On most tops, supporting bows are used to shape the top and hold it up between main bows. Often, pockets like headliner listing strips are used for these auxiliary bows. Usually the bows are removed by undoing them and sliding them out of the pockets. Newer convertibles have a two-piece

Fig. 11-7. Late 1930s Pontiac convertible top with snaps to hold sides of top covering in place, a typical convertible of the era.

unit, the inner section slipping into the pocket and an outer section attaching to it with screws.

PADS AND BOWS

Examine the top pads after the covering is removed. If they are torn and worn, replace them. They can be fluffed up and, if necessary, stuffed with more cotton padding. On many convertibles, the pads position the rear bow, which is not connected directly to the rest of the top framework. If the pads are loose or stretched, the rear bow may be leaning too far rearward. You can check the fit of the rear bow by positioning your new top over the framework and approximating the tacking strip above the rear bow. There should be enough material at the front to adequately tack and enough material extending at the lower edges to work with.

To bring the rear bow more upright, untack the pads one at a time at the front header bow and draw the rear bow forward. To lower it toward the rear, loosen the quarter stay pads and use them to effect the adjustment.

Factory literature will sometimes give proper measurements for positioning the rear bow. The most important of these is usually taken from a straight line running from the back edge of the rear bow to the lip of the body opening. The measurement is made about 1½-inches in from the ends of the bow. Even if you do not know the correct figure, you can at least make sure the bow is an equal number of inches away from the body opening on each side.

NEW REAR CURTAIN

Putting in the rear window curtain is the first operation of installing the new top. There are at least four styles of rear curtains but the most common type is the all-around zipper curtain. It is found with the older small glass windows, in most plastic window cars, and in modern convertibles with flexible glass windows (Fig. 11-8).

If your car is an older convertible without removable trim sticks, you start the rear curtain by centering it on the rear bow and tacking out from the center. The metal zipper track should be at least ¾-inch below the bow so it will work without interference.

Pull the lower edge of the curtain down as tight as possible and center it on the rear trim rail. Starting at the center again, space out three of four tracks each way. Stay-tack so you can adjust if need be. Next, tack the zipper flaps to the rear bow. These have the zipper sewn into them. Keep them in line with the back curtain so the zippers will work easily. Work the zipper back and forth to check the alignment and adjust as required. A bit of extra patience here will save many hours of fighting a stubborn zipper later. Once you are satisfied with the zipper's operation, drive all tacks home.

Convertible rear curtains on cars with newer-style trim sticks are installed in a completely different manner. This time you start by stay-tacking the curtain to the center piece of trim stick. Align the edge flush with the bottom of the trim stick so it will be straight. Tack out to what would be just beyond the edge of the window insert. Place your tacks close to screws, and don't forget to open holes in the fabric for their installation. Trim sticks are metal with insets of pressed cardboard. Before you get too far in replacing the top, make sure they are still serviceable.

Use a tack to suspend the curtain assembly from the rear bow and attach the trim stick. If you removed the quarter stay pads, reinstall at this time, carefully smoothing them.

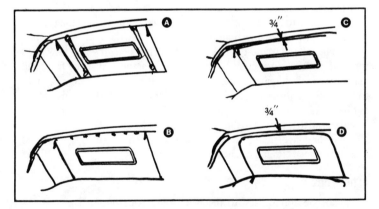

Fig. 11-8. Four common styles of rear curtain window assemblies are shown. A) Zippers hold curtain on side edges, straps supply tension; B) Zippers on edges and fasteners across top edge hold this style in place; C) Three zipper style uses zippers up each edge and separate zipper across top; D) All-around zipper style is frequently used on larger plastic windows, too. Zipper track starts at lower right corner, crosses above window and goes down left side. Three zipper and all-around zippers need at least ¾-inch clearance from rear bow to clear.

Pull the curtain up to the rear bow all across, stretching it to remove fullness and wrinkles. Tack to the rear bow and trim off excess (Fig. 11-9).

TOPS WITH WELTS

After the curtain is installed, the top is ready to go on. On older cars a single cord welt is installed around the rear trim and along the front edge of the header bow. This is 1-inch welting with a rope-like core. The welt has a gummed surface that goes down on the trim rail or up on the header. It is tacked at 6- to 8-inch intervals. Make sure the fully-colored side is visible to you. To finish the ends of the welt, allow about 1½-inches overhang on each end. Open the material and cut off the beading. Fold the empty flap under the still-beaded welt and tack.

Place the new top material on the car and snap it down wherever possible. Older convertibles have two styles of tops that are tacked the rear bow in different manners. The valance style of top has a separate valance trim piece that tacks right above the rear bow. The other type has a flap of top material which is tacked over the rear curtain frame material.

On valance-equipped tops, stay-tack at the outside corners of the rear bow after aligning and smoothing the top. Then go the front of the car and pull the material forward and down, letting the side quarters fall into their place along the side roof rails. Stay-tack the front bow. Check the clearance of the top by opening and closing doors with windows up. If the clearance is only slightly inadequate, the top can be raised by building up the pads. Move to the rear again and tack the quarter sections to the rear bow. Then, smooth them carefully and tack to the trim rail. Stay-tack in case later alignment is required. Then, center the valance and tack it along the upper edge to the rear bow. Finish the rear bow by tacking the top flap to the valance for a weathertight seal.

To install the frame-type top, begin tacking along the rear bow after top is smoothed and centered. Pull the material forward at the front and stay tack. Tack the quarters as described in the section on valance-style tops. Then tack the rear curtain frame's upper edge to the bow—don't tack out beyond its edges. Bring the top flap down and tack it over the curtain frame and all the way out to the edges of the bow.

Newer convertible tops are made without a flap at the rear bow and thus do not need either a valance or curtain frame flap.

OLDER TOPS

The operations used to install an older car top are considerably different from those for mid-1950s and newer cars. We'll review the completion of the older top installation first, followed by a description of the finishing operation on a newer-style top.

To finish off the older style at the front, trim excess material so it is flush with the single cord welting we installed earlier. The binding along the sides of the top will extend forward and down. Trim along the upper

Fig. 11-9. Metal rear window frames for glass panes are installed without opening being cut in material. After installation, fabric is trimmed out with a sharp knife.

edge of the binding back to where it intersects with the header bow tacking, then cut the "V" shaped piece of material. Pull the beading around the corner of the header bow and tack it to the front trim rail.

Then, re-install the rear side window weather strips. The top side flaps fit in between their metal retainers and the top frame. Install the holding screws and work the rubber weather strip back into its channel.

Carefully check the top at this point for smoothness and alignment. Canvas tops will smooth out small wrinkles by themselves after being wet a few times. Make adjustments as necessary, then drive all tacks home.

Wire-on binding is used to cover the exposed tacking on the front and rear bows. Spacing tacks every inch, tack the binding on, with the round head on the lower edge. Keep the wire-on in a straight line for good appearance. Then fold the flat section of the wire-on binding down to cover the tacks.

Chrome welting tips finish the top. One goes on each end of the wire-on binding on the front bow and one on each end of the wire-on across the rear bow tacking line. A final pair are installed at the ends of the wire-on binding used to finish the rear trim rail.

NEWER TOPS

To install a top on a mid-1950s or newer convertible, you will need trimmer's cement. Begin by folding in the rear weather flaps at the rear curtain. Line the top up at the rear curtain top. Cement the rear-quarter flaps at the frame rails near the side windows. Stay tack the top at the rear bow, aligning the seams on the bow as you work.

Pull the top material forward so it is relatively snug and cement the front corner flaps to their proper places on the top frame rails. Don't make the top too tight right now. The tension will be drawn later.

Go to the rear and loosen the center trim stick. Push the top material down between the trim stick and the body. Align the top material and install enough screws through the trim stick and material to keep in place. Then, with the top latched, go to the front and pull the fabric tight to remove fullness. While holding the fabric taut, have someone else mark the underside of the fabric at the front rail.

Unlock the top and raise the frame. Apply cement to the underside of the rail and to the top material. Cement the top material to the rail, aligning it with the chalk line your helper made. Let it dry and check the fit, latching the top to check tension. When you're happy with the fit, unlatch the top and tack the material on the underside of the bow.

Install the header weather strip. Go back the rear bow and, without pulling too tight, remove excess fullness and stay-tack the top at the rear bow. Go over the whole job once more to make sure everything is centered and aligned, then drive the tacks in. This tacking will need to be sealed. Flow the sealant around the tacks to do the job thoroughly. For added insurance, seal this strip on the inside, too.

Do not tack too far beyond the seam on the rear bow because all tacks will be covered by the wire-on binding. If your car had tension wires to control side pull-up, install the wires in the new top by leading them through on a flexible wire.

Mark the fabric along the upper edge of the trim stick, then loosen the stick and remove it from the body. Using the marks, tack the material permanently to the stick, then re-install.

Inside the car, draw the quarter sections down and mark them, using their trim sticks for guides. Remove the quarter section trim sticks and tack the quarters to them. Check all alignments one more time after you fit the quarter trim sticks in and attach them with a holding screw or two.

To seal the trim sticks, apply sealing tape to their faces after the material is tacked. This forms a seal between the top material and the body lip.

After sealing tape is applied, the trim sticks can be attached for the last time. Cover the tacks on the rear bow with wire-on molding, using "Hidem" tips to finish the binding ends.

Installing a new top boot is easy, of course. It slips into the channel along the rear upper edge of the back seat on most convertibles, then snaps down around the edges.

You can sew up a new top boot yourself, using the old one for a pattern. The worst problem will be accounting for shrinkage, especially on the vinyl boots. Much trial fitting may be required to develop your patterns. Salvage the snaps from the old boot, if possible. A trimmer with access to wholesale suppliers can help you replace the snaps if they are needed.

FABRIC TOP INSERTS

It is almost a certainty that any car you own built before 1936 will need the rubberized roof insert replaced. Installing a new insert isn't an impossible job and we will review a typical installation. Usually the biggest problem is not with the covering but in repairing the wood rot that comes to light when the old covering is removed. On cars with wood body framing, the top insert is one of the most important keys to preserving the car. It must be watertight.

To replace a top, you must first remove the crown molding, the strip that covers the edges of the top insert. Use a bent screwdriver or chisel to pry the molding up, getting leverage with a wooden block. Be careful not to exert so much pressure that the sheet metal roof side panels are damaged. The molding is hard to find, too, so try not to bend it too badly.

Remove the tacks in the channel under the crown molding and undo the top fabric, if it is present. Under the padding you will find chicken wire, wooden slats and the upper side of the headliner. This is as good a time as any to take care of wood problems.

Scrape the old cement off the metal ledges where the roof covering was tacked. You will find slotted holes along the rim of the metal side panels, through which the tacks were driven. Marking the centers of these slots will help align the new top.

STARTING THE NEW ROOF

If needed, install new padding for the roof. Cut the new roof material with about three inches extra length, but cut to the correct width. Apply a good sealant to the tacking rails and let it set.

Stretch the new roof material over the opening, dividing the extra three inches front and rear. Stay tack at the centers of the front and rear panels, using 6 or 8 oz. trimmers tacks. Then, stretch the fabric and stay tack one of the back corners, followed by the diagonal front corner, and then do the other corners. Check the alignment and make sure the lines grained into the top are running true. Tack across the rear panel. Stay tack the sides and align everything again, then tack the front rail. Finish by tacking the sides, lifting the roof material to locate the slots as you go. Drive your tacks into the close end of each slot.

Crown moldings were installed in three sections, but replacements were always supplied in four straight pieces to facilitate shipping. Nail the front section on first, using one-inch molding nails through the slots. Start at the center and work out to the drip moldings. Saw off the excess with a hacksaw. Use a nail set to drive the nails. The crown molding is made like wire-on upholstery binding. The nails are hidden by the upper strip which is folded over onto the nailing strip. To do this correctly, you need a swage tool. This is shaped to the contour of the molding cap strip and used with a wooden mallet to close the strip. It is tricky to get the molding level but it pays off to be patient.

Do the side strips after the front strip, starting at the rear curve and working forward. Attach the rear crown strip and finish off the ends of all strips. Cut off excess top material with a sharp knife and seal the new insert carefully with a sealant-cement on the inner edge of the molding.

LANDAU TOPS

Until about 1932 most sport model closed cars had full leatherette, or in some cases, genuine leather, roof coverings. These styles often had landau irons to give the appearance of a convertible, just like modern vinyl tops are designed to do.

Restoring one of these tops is a difficult job for the amateur restorer but it can be done. Right off you will have to make a pattern for the four pieces that make up a full roof covering. These are a roof insert, as we have described, a back panel for around the rear window, and rear quarter sections with arms running forward to cover the sheet metal roof side panels.

The quarter panels are often formed with pre-shaped board. Padding is cemented to the board and the fabric goes on over it. Tacking the full-padded roof is too complex to get into here. Unless original top service information is available, deduce your procedure from the removal of the old top. The top section seams are covered with binding to finish the job.

Chapter 12
Sealing The Car

Many hours of labor and many dollars are sewn into a restored car's interior. But what will happen if this splendid new upholstery is exposed to water and weather? The results can be disastrous. Water can wreck a closed car interior. This chapter will help detect potential problems and suggest how to solve them to preserve a car's interior.

If you have a convertible, you don't have to worry as much as the closed car owner. Leather and its imitations are durable and water will not hurt them if reasonable care is taken. A dry cloth can be used to wipe off the drops that get on the interior when you are frantically putting up the top. Extra careful installation of the header bar weather strip is especially important to keep convertibles dry. The top seams may require sealing, as discussed in Chapter 11.

Vent window rubber seals are often a source of serious leakage. Vent window seals for some popular cars are available from hobby centers. They are rather expensive, but well worth the cost. This is one item not to be found in usable condition in a salvage yard. Reproducing these is a possibility, but very expensive. One restorer reported an expenditure of more than $300 plus hours of labor to make new seals for his 1935 convertible.

A treatment with one of the new rubber and vinyl rejuvenators should prolong the life of original seals if they are still intact.

Closed cars are very susceptible to water damage. You probably replaced the headliner because it was water-stained and yellowed. The carpet is probably water-rotted and the lower edges of the kick panels all but dissolved. On the dash and garnish moldings, seepage through the window seals no doubt has left tracks across the woodgrain or paint.

Obviously, water has no place inside a freshly restored sedan. But it is almost a certainty that a car has developed leaks over the years. Without using a hose, we'll try to locate some of them.

FIRST, THE OPENINGS

Start sealing the car at the door openings and around windows. These rubber seals not only waterproof but keep wind and dust out, too. Finding suitable gaskets often requires much detective work but sometimes a modern section with the right contour can be found.

Glass Seal, made by GE, is recommended for sealing windshields suffering from a loose or deteriorated weatherstrip. You have to get the sealant right down to the point where the glass touches the rubber strip to make an effective seal. *Don't* use epoxy here—it is not resilient enough for use between rubber and metal or glass.

On pre-1936 cars with roof inserts the top should be thoroughly sealed both to prevent the upholstery from being damaged and to preserve the wood body bracing.

Inspect the top for cracking, tears or holes. The best remedy is to install a new insert as detailed in Chapter 11. This is a lot cheaper than buying a roof section of wood.

In the event the insert is serviceable, proceed with sealing it. As you know from the last chapter, it was originally sealed along the inner lip of the crown molding with molding cement. This is probably cracked and curling with age. Scrape it out and reseal with a modern compound.

Inspect the drip moldings, too. The car's paint was supposed to seal them where they contact roof panels. But shrinkage and vibration over the years may crack the paint allowing water to seep in and creep through the nailing slots into your precious wood. Use sealant on the drip moldings and when the car is repainted ask the painter to make sure they are sealed with paint when the paint job is finished.

OTHER POINTS OF ENTRY

Other areas of wood-framed bodies that should be carefully checked include: the open joints at the top and bottom of the sheet metal covers for the front body pillars; the weather strip retainer channel on the lower edge of the windshield; and door weather strips. Use a rubber dough sealant for these jobs.

On many 1920s cars raised moldings on the body were nailed on instead of rolled right into the metal like later cars. They were installed with sealant and, of course, further sealed by the paint. Like drip moldings, they may leak because the paint has pulled away or cracked, letting in water.

To reset loose moldings, make a swage tool and renail them. Be sure they are resealed when the car is repainted.

Windlace or windhose is supposed to be part of the seal against water but remember, it is covered with fabric, too, and subject to deterioration. The doors should be sealed by weather strips, not windlace.

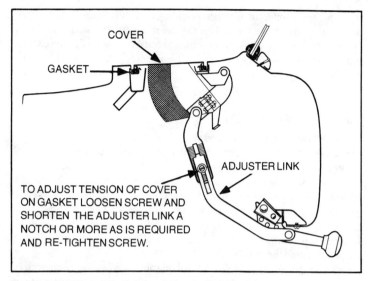

COVER

GASKET

ADJUSTER LINK

TO ADJUST TENSION OF COVER ON GASKET LOOSEN SCREW AND SHORTEN THE ADJUSTER LINK A NOTCH OR MORE AS IS REQUIRED AND RE-TIGHTEN SCREW.

Fig. 12-1. Location of cowl vent gasket and adjustable link.

The Famous Cowl Leak

If you've owned many older cars, you've probably had the following irritation. Driving along in a pouring rain, you've had to put up with slow-moving vacuum wipers, steamed windshields, and all the nuts skidding around who magically appear with the first drops of rain. But the final straw is the older car's habit of dripping cold water onto your right foot (Fig. 12-1).

A wet right foot is usually attributable to one of Detroit's most long-lived features, the cowl vent. Finally, in the late 1940's, they remedied the cold foot problem with a water-collecting device called the plenum chamber. But, if your car has one of the old flip-up cowl vents, you're probably going to get wet unless you carefully seal and adjust the vent.

Vent gaskets for the cowl are still easily found; they can be ordered from mail order houses and reproduction specialists. Cowl vent gaskets also have a surprising degree of universality. Some manufacturers used one gasket on all their makes for periods of several years.

The cowl vent gasket is cemented in place. Remove the old gasket and thoroughly clean the channel it fits into. Using sealant-cement, install the new gasket.

The cover is adjustable by loosening the hinge arm bolts. It can be shifted to better contact the gasket. Under the dash, follow the operating lever up into the area under the cowl. Most will have an adjuster link, similar to a turn buckle, in their hookup. Loosen the lock screw and shorten the link a bit to put more tension on the cover against the seal. The lever latches through an over-center spring, probably, so don't shorten the link a bit to put more tension on the cover against the seal. The lever latches through an over-center spring, probably, so don't shorten the linkage so much you have to force the lever unduly. Check the seal now by inserting a piece of paper at intervals around the vent cover, then closing the lid. If the paper slips out, you still have problems.

Trim, Molding, Window Leaks

Most two- and four-door sedans built from the later 1930s through the mid-1950s share leakage problems. Some of the most common sources of water damage in these cars are as follows:

If a car has been repainted during its life, there is a chance the chrome trim strips may not have been resealed at the trim clip holes.

On cars with chrome moldings that follow the curve of the top around to the rear window on the lower edge, watch for evidence of leakage at the lower rear lip of the trunk floor. Water will follow the inside panels of the trunk down onto the floor.

This type of leak is sealed by applying auto body sealer compound to the trim clip holes. Auto body sealer is also used on glass edges, floor pans, tail light openings and other similar areas. The other major type of sealer is weather strip cement used to hold rubber or glass to metal.

Before sealing window gaskets, renew them with a rubber treatment to stop deterioration and give them a nice healthy sheen.

Then take a sealing gun, load with body sealer and work it down between the gasket and glass, running a bead around the gasket. If the leak or deterioration is so bad that you must replace the gasket, use the sealer in the channel before installing the glass for extra caution. After the sealant is installed, change to cement and apply to the inner edge of the gasket lip near the top, cementing it to the glass.

Sometimes a leak at the base of the front door vent window can't be adjusted out. Remove the door garnish molding and trim assembly. Place waterproof cardboard shims under the section where contact is made with the lower edge of the vent window frame.

You can also adjust the angle of contact on the rear upright weatherstrip. Use the same trick described for checking the cowl vent—a piece of paper slipped out means you've still got a leak.

Door Leaks

On the door itself remove "live" weather strip to readjust if need be. It is usually glued and clipped into place. Use great caution and patience in removing it. Before doing this, though, try slightly moving the door latch striker plate just a hair to draw the door tighter against the strip. This may cure the problem.

When re-installing weather strip, make sure the channel it fits into is very clean. The strip should be molded to fit the door, so do not stretch it.

112

While re-installing or putting on new weather strip you'll notice small drain holes, often notched or rectangular openings, in the lower or bottom edge of the door. These should be cleaned out and kept free of muck and blockages. Don't block them with your new weather strip.

These drains carry water that comes down between window glass and weather stripping, plus whatever streams in through the trim holes.

Other areas that may need resealing on a car include the following:

Hinge, Trunk, Quarter-Window Leaks

Hinge plates should be sealed where they bolt to the body. On some cars an access plate was installed. It should be sealed, too. Place the sealant at the top and bottom of the hinge plates' outer ends. If there is an access plate, remove it and run sealer around its backside edges.

The decklid weather strip is a frequent source of trunk leakage and damage. A new strip should be available from one of the sources we've mentioned. Clean out the gutter and repair rust if need be before installing a new strip. Use your faithful piece of paper to check the tightness of the seal.

Many older sedans have a rear quarter window, a third window behind the rear door, sort of like a modern "opera" window. These usually were hinged to swing in or out. To drain off water that seeped or leaked through quarter window gaskets, body engineers installed a pan or cup with a drain hose running down to a drain hole in the rocker panel bottom edge (Fig. 12-2).

If any part of the quarter window drainage system is plugged, rusted or rotted, you may be shocked to find dampness spreading down the

Fig. 12-2. Reproduction rear door vent window seals help keep this 1938 Cadillac 60-S interior preserved in all its restored elegance.

quarter trim panels and onto the back seat and rear floor carpet. Sometimes the water seems to be coming from under the seat assembly.

To repair the drain system the back seat assembly and quarter trim panels must be removed. Patch obvious leaks. If nothing shows, check the pinchweld seam on the drain pan. This was a great source of trouble on some cars, even when they were new. Replace the drain hose if it is cracked or hardened. Use cement to attach the hose and make sure, again, those pinchwelds are waterproof.

To check the drain system for clogging, remove the quarter window garnish molding and use a flashlight to look down into the drain pit. Clean the pan out with a suitable implement. A wire can be used to open the drain tube. Flush with water to make sure the problem is solved.

FINDING LEAK SOURCES

Leaks are often hard to trace since water may flow along inner sheet metal, finally emerging onto your interior far from where it entered the car body. Anywhere a hole has been punched in the exterior sheet metal is a potential source of water leakage. When painting a car, a good bit of insurance is to seal every bolt and clip.

Sometimes water isn't draining *down* into your interior, it is coming *up* into it. Rusty floorboards are the most common cause of this sort of leakage. But even perfectly preserved cars sometimes leak from below.

The floor pan on many cars is made up of sections. Water may be forced through gaps in the spot welds by wind and wheel spray. It will show up on the underside of your carpet.

The weld joints can be sealed with sealing compound. Clean them thoroughly first, of course. Many cars can be sealed from above, too.

On cars with an inner fender panel crimped and welded to the body structure, water may leak through and flow out onto your carpet, then soak up into the quarter panel and lower skirt of the back seat. These welds can be sealed with compound, too, and should be.

Doing sealing operations while body work is in progress can save much time and disappointment later. It is another good reason for completing the rest of a restoration before doing the interior.

Chapter 13
Protection and Care

A freshly-restored interior should be well cared for so it will not have to be replaced again for a long time. Back in the old days when you bought a car, a nice little book of many pages came with it. This book lived in the glove compartment. It was called the "owner's manual." Among other things it told how to maintain the interior. Any used car clean-up man could attest no one ever read the little book. Detroit seems to have got the message because in many new cars the owner's manual has vanished, replaced by a single leaf fact sheet.

In fairness, it must be said modern cars are easier to maintain. Simply ignore them in most cases until something goes wrong. Then, you are supposed to trade them in. But some stubborn souls continue to maintain their cars. Modern interiors are easily cared for. A good aerosol cleaner, sponge and a towel to rub dry will clean up years of grime in a jiffy on most post-1960 interiors.

Abrasive polishes, good for a quick polish, will harm just about any surface on your car except the engine block. Stay away from them and do the job right with elbow grease.

For car interiors dating to the days of fabric trim, we have gleaned some old, but still valid, tips for cleaning and maintaining the interior. You may recognize some of them as being the same words in your dad's owner's manual when you were a kid.

UPHOLSTERY CARE—FLAT AND PILE FABRICS

Flat trim, as we know, is flat. So, its whole surface is subject to fading, discoloration and grime. Flat trim is usually harder to clean than pile fabrics. Piles catch dirt on their nap, breaking it up and keeping it off the backing surface. Don't forget, though, the rubberized backing may fade away if you hit it with too strong a cleaner. Boarded trim, too, deserves special consideration. You must not saturate the fabric with so much fluid that it dampens and warps or otherwise damages the fiberboard backing.

The following suggestions are for new upholstery. Old trim fades and discolors so much that any work you do on it will leave a bright clean spot standing out. Too, fabric weakens with age, while stains and grime get more set as time passes.

To remove an unidentified stain, first try a clean cloth, non-alkaline soap and warm water. Don't use bleach. It weakens the material and will probably do the job too well by removing coloration.

When you're out touring, a spark plug fouls, and you gash your hand on a head bolt removing it. You're sure to get some blood on the upholstery just for good measure.

Rub the spots with a cold water-soaked rag, changing frequently to clean sections of the rag. If this doesn't work, apply a bit of household ammonia cleaner to the spot, let sit for a moment and then go to it again with the rag. If the spot persists, it is likely set for good. Your only recourse is to start a rumor your car was once owned by the Dillinger gang.

Candy And Ice Cream

Someday you will have to let the junior members of the family and their friends into the car. They often display lack of tact by eating candy in the car, some of which, no doubt, will work its way onto your upholstery.

If the offending candy was non-chocolate, rub the spot with a rag wet with very hot water. Keep the hot water treatment very brief and don't let the moisture move out onto non-affected areas of the upholstery. A drop of carbon tetrachloride will remove residue.

To remove a chocolate creme spot, use a cloth soaked in lukewarm soap suds, scraping the surface while wet with a knife. Rinse by rubbing with a cold water-soaked rag.

Pure chocolate is best removed with luke-warm water, followed by sponging the area with carbon-tetrachloride or similar solution.

For ice cream, use the hot water treatment, followed by a warm soap suds application if need be. Rinse with cold water. Good old carbon tetrachloride will clear out the stain.

If your female companion becomes so carried away with nostalgia that lipstick somehow gets on the upholstery, try carbon tetrachloride. Then try blotting the stain with blotting paper. If it still persists, you have a permanent mark on your interior.

Water spots can be minimized by sponging the entire panel or section afflicted with cold water and a cloth.

Battery Acid, Mildew, Grease

Should battery acid contact your interior and if you happen to have a box of baking soda or a bottle of household ammonia in your hand, douse the acid, quick. If you have to run in the house to get either of these, you might as well forget it. It will be too late when you get back. Even if the fabric does not appear to be damaged, the acid will eat into it during the course of a few days. Too, it will eat right through the foam or padding under the covering. Acid on upholstery is a disaster.

Fresh mildew stains might come off with a vigorous rub down using a warm soap suds solution. Rinse by cold water applied on a cloth. Old mildew will come off, too, but usually spots badly. An old remedy for mildew stains called for using a 10% oxalic acid solution right on the spot, letting it stand for a moment. After blotting dry with paper or cloth, a cold water rinse was poured on the area—best done with fabric removed, of course!

Grease spots will come off mohair or other pile fabrics without too much difficulty, since it is usually out on the ends of the pile unless it gets ground in. Using a mild cleaning fluid, start on the outside of the spotted area and work in. Repeat several times, always rotating your cloth to clean areas. Working from inside out instead of outside in increases the probability of an edge ring or discoloration. After the fabric is completely dry, brush it thoroughly with a whisk broom.

Mohair can be laundered with soap and water using a mild neutral soap. Apply suds with a sponge or brush rubbing with the pile. Dry by wiping surface repeatedly with dry cloth. Drying is aided by brushing with a clean whisk broom, circulating air through the nap. Brush again when the material is dried thoroughly.

LEATHER CARE

Dust is the most serious threat to the conscientious owner of a leather-interiored car. It is harmful both as an abrasive and chemically. The ideal way to remove dust is by suction, a chore handily accomplished with a shop vacuum. Keep the suction tip a fraction of an inch above the surface. Further protect your investment in hide by washing it occasionally (always remove dust first!) with a light non-detergent castile soap. Buff it dry to a nice soft glow. Be sure to avoid cleaners with any sort of abrasive content. Both real and imitation leathers can be seriously damaged by abrasive particles.

Annual or periodic applications of a leather treatment may keep the material pliable and soft. Hobby suppliers offer a number of treatments. Avoid harsh chemical compounds.

Chapter 14
An Interior
Restoration Teacher Speaks

There are, of course, mail order upholstery courses. These teach basic upholstery techniques as they apply to both home furniture and automotive applications. Then, there are those evening upholstery classes at your local junior college. Here, the basic orientation is toward furniture—you might be able to work on cushions if the instructor is willing to go along. There is only one full-time college that offers a course in automotive interior restoration, that we know of. That school is McPherson College, in McPherson, Kansas.

This centrally located school offers a unique two year automotive restoration course. During each semester a Model A Ford and Ford Mustang are restored from the ground up, including full interior renovation. Freshman students work on a car upholstered with a kit, while sophomores construct an interior from scratch, making and fitting the upholstery from yard goods. During an annual interterm project, a Model T Ford touring car is restored in four weeks, with the interior being made and installed as part of the project. A top kit is used for that facet of the restoration.

Jim Willems, head instructor for the McPherson College program is an experienced restorer well acquainted with automotive trimming and its problems and rewards.

THE HARD PARTS

The author asked Jim Willems what the most difficult part of McPherson College's interior restoration classes was for the students. "I would say the actual fitting and sewing," he replied. "As far as spring repair, good instruction can get almost anybody by. Padding a trim assembly is also easily learned, Willems said, unless the restorer is dealing with a car whose cushions have rotted down to bare springs. "Most students have no idea how much padding is required or what type of padding is required; many do not realize that burlap is needed, for instance, to keep cotton from filtering down into the springs". He suggests basic furniture upholstery texts for insights into the amount of padding to use.

McPherson students are intructed to always do the interior trimming after the exterior paintwork is completed on the vehicle. "You might make some preparation before the painting is done," Willems suggests, however, " . . . like in the case of cars with trim sticks—they use a metal C-type strip with hard paper in it for holding tacks, and it was welded to the body. These strips should be replaced or fitted before repainting is done or you'll mess up the paint later. But all the actual trimming and nailing is done after the painting," Willems said.

"You'll be painting inside and out," Willems cautions. Floorboards will be stripped, repaired and painted before any interior work can begin.

KITS FOR THE FORTUNATE

Jim Willems has high praise for the upholstery kits he has used, although most have required some alteration, especially top kits. The school has used top kits on their Model T Ford interterm projects with good results, and they have done several Mustangs with kits.

"I would advise anyone who isn't proficient in restoration to get one of these kits if they are available," Willems said, adding, "It's cheaper for one thing. You can buy a kit for very little more than all the material will cost you because when you start buying material you have to buy larger pieces of material than you need." Not only will you need these over-sized pieces to cut your pattern pieces from, but many items that come with the kit are cut to size, whereas burlap will have to be purchased in quanity from a retailer. A minimum purchase is often required—Willems said that you might have to buy 10 yards of burlap as a minimum, for instance, and a lot of it will end up on your garage floor and rafters (Fig. 14-1).

WHERE DO WE BEGIN?

We asked Jim Willems what sort of car a beginner should tackle if he isn't going to be able to obtain a kit. "I really wouldn't advise a beginner to do a high dollar classic car," he said, "That would be a false economy." Willems says a simple closed car is a good place to start, if a kit isn't available. An Essex or Chevrolet with cloth interior, for instance, would be a good "first car."

"Of course, sedans are the most difficult *body style* to do," Willems said, "as far as the headliner and door panels." Still, such a car is a good beginner's project, since it probably had a cloth interior. "Cloth is much easier to work with than vinyl or leather. Cloth is very forgiving. If you mess up you simply undo it and start all over," Willems advised. Vinyl isn't so easily retacked or sewn. Once it has stitch tracks in it or nail holes that show, the restorer will have to start over with a new piece of material.

A further advantage of cloth, Jim Willems said, is that "it will stretch a little in both directions, while most vinyls will stretch in one direction. You can get expanded vinyl now, which of course was not available originally, and it is a little more forgiving. The old leatherette, though, was simply a light canvas with a synthetic waterproof covering over it. It does not stretch at all."

GETTING THE GOODS

Willems told the author that basic trimming supplies are "easily obtained." He suggests trim shops or furniture supply stores as good places to shop. He also pointed out that many trimmers have gone into the retail goods business, buying from their sources wholesale, in bulk, for retail sale. Such trimmers will have access to the wholesale firms that would turn down your small retail order. Willems said that items such as tacks or thread might be obtained most reasonably and quickly through a friendly local trimmer. "In most cases they will sell you what you need, or if they don't have it they will order for you," he says.

ABOUT GRAINING

Speaking about woodgraining with Di Noc and other pressure-sensitive materials, Willems said he has found them increasingly hard to obtain. He tries to match the grain he has in mind to a late model "woodie" station wagon, then orders a whole repair panel of the material from the dealer handling that line. Not all pressure-sensitive materials are flexible, Willems cautioned. He also reminded that using detergent to form a film between the surface and the Di Noc material is essential while positioning is done. The latest type bonds instantly to the surface when the soap is squeezed out with a squeegee, so extra care must be taken during alignment.

ON THE CARPET

Frequently a hobbyist restorer's first attempt at upholstery is the replacement of a worn or ragged carpet in an otherwise nice car. This seemingly simple job can turn into a recurring nightmare. Jim Willems spends considerable time teaching students at McPherson College the correct method of installing a carpet so that it stays in place. Willems told the author that so-called "molded carpet" sets are the easiest and best ways to go, if they are available. These are offered for some of the more popular collector cars, such as Ford's Mustang and Thunderbirds, plus an increasing number of Chevrolets from the 1950's and '60s. The other type of carpet kit, which Willems refers to as "tailored" is a flat piece of material cut on a pattern and stitched where necessary to give it the contour of the floor panel. To install these carpets so that they do not come loose and

Fig. 14-1. Camaros are benefiting from their popularity as reproduction suppliers see the volume necessary to make reproduction interior parts economically feasible. Would-be auto trimmers are advised to start with a car for which kits are available.

creep, Willems recommended using spray cement all around the edges, spraying the adhesive both on the carpet backing and the floor panel. Don't use the spray cement where the carpet lays on a jute backing, though, such as over the floor tunnel.

"A tailored carpet doesn't look like it will fit at all to start with," Willems said, adding, "A carpet that has been folded up for a long time may look very discouraging and shabby at first." By using spray cement the carpeting can be shaped to fit. The cement remains tacky indefinitely, allowing you to stick down one side of the carpet, work it across to the other side, and, if you come up half an inch off, lift the carpet easily and stick it down again in the new position.

ATTACHING THE CARPET

"When you are all finished with the fitting you should nail or screw the carpet down," Willems tells his students.

Many later model cars already have screw-type carpet fasteners. Self-tapping screws hold the carpet down at six to ten locations, (usually four under the front seat, one in each upper front corner and two in back). "I'd suggest using a few more," Willems said, "Most of the problems I've seen with carpet replacement result from the carpet not being fastened down. You start using the car and the carpet starts pulling out from under the door sill plates and then, of course, it starts bagging. Soon it is all out of shape. So it should be glued down all around the edge." Willems uses special drive screws for carpet installations. These are screws with a long taper that are started and turned down with hammer blows. Self-tapping, phillips-head screws with washers are also frequently used. Willems uses black or dark colored screws in most carpets so they are invisible to the eye when in place.

Long experience has made Jim Willems a very practical teacher. "Do not drills holes to start these screws," he tells his students when explaining how to fasten a carpet down. "If you drill a hole in the floor all you've got holding your screw is the thickness of the metal." By starting the screw with a hammer or making a pilot hole with an awl Willems says that you, "roll all that metal down and have two or three threads catching." Further, he warns, do not drill through a carpet for any reason. "Anyone drilling a hole through a carpet will catch one of the threads on the bit and it will cause a run just like in an old silk stocking."

Drive screws can be obtained from a local trim shop. To remove them from a car, tap them from the bottom and they will turn themselves out. Use a self-tapping screw to replace the carpet. "When puncturing holes make sure they are not going into a frame area or double-sheeted area—like on a Mustang where the frame is under the side sill area," Willems cautions. If you must place a fastener in such an area, drill the hole. To avoid drilling through the carpet, mark the floor pan with an ice pick or awl through the carpet, then lift it to drill the hole. On older cars with flat floors and carpets, the carpeting will tend to push toward the center of the floor, Willems said. They should be fastened down, too. The only cars that Jim Willems does not fasten carpeting down on are very early cars whose floors are completely flat and whose carpets were virtually throw rugs—designed to be taken out and shaken to clean when they were dirty.

USING THE WATER SHIELD

Turning to door panels, Jim Willems says that he always installs some type of water shield between the trim panel and the door itself. This shield can be made of plastic sheeting, heavy waxed paper, or any water repellent material. Don't use something like felt paper, though. Willems installs door shields on all cars, even Model A Fords, whether they originally had them or not. Modern cars come with a specially-treated paper seal. But, as Willems pointed out, many mechanics remove the seal while servicing door mechanisms and window lifts. As often as not they do not replace the seal. "That's why so many doors are eaten out from rust," Willems said. Dampness will also cause boarded door panels to buckle and warp from the mositure and may even cause discoloration of the interior trim panel.

"The waterproof shield can be glued to the door with butyl caulking or something similar," Willems told the author. It should be stuck to the door, not the trim panel. Use the door as a pattern, not the trim panel. Otherwise, you may get visible ragged edges when the panel is installed. When applying adhesive at the bottom of the door be sure you leave the channels to the drain holes open, Willems cautioned.

Fig. 14-2. Installation problems vary from car to car. New dash pad for Mustang is relatively simple, could be a nightmare on a car such as this Thunderbird.

DASH PADS

Installing a dash pad can be a pleasant, easy task for the beginning upholster, or it can be a real headache, Jim Willems tells his students. It all depends on the car—some can even drive a professional up the wall. Deteriorated dash pads are a problem with many collector cars. For the lucky owners of very popular collector cars such as Corvettes and Mustangs there is instant relief through the purchase of ready-made dash pad kits. But even these may be difficult to install. For cars without kits, Willems suggests searching salvage yards for a good, uncracked dash pad. Such a pad from a junked car may be repainted with a good vinyl paint to match your car's interior.

On some cars the installation can be a "terrible job," Willems said. 1958-1960 Thunderbirds (Fig. 14-2) are especially difficult, he says, "You have to practically disassemble the entire interior on these. You have to take the seats out, the console out, radio out, all the instruments and half the wiring, but it can be done."

Willems has successfully tailored a pad to fit cars for which a reproduction or usable pad from a junked car could not be obtained. The tailored pad, since it isn't molded, will usually require a double-stitched seam where the pad starts down the vertical face of the instrument panel (some early dash pads were made this way, in fact). The double stitch is made by sewing the two pieces of the dash pad together, then sewing through the material to a piece of fabric tape, backing the seam on each side of the original seam. This reinforces the seam and keeps it from separating. Willems also tailors bulge type armrests in this manner where the original used molded vinyl.

LOOKS THE SAME

Sometimes, Willems said, the restorer can substitute one sort of material for another in a tough restoration job. "In the case of a trim panel

123

which had skinny plastic trim strips that were plated and are peeling; you could actually replace the strips with small, thin aluminum moldings which you might find in a salvage yard. You can form these moldings to come very close to matching the trim on panels." The plastic strips are usually heat welded to the door panels and cannot be removed without destroying them. The ideal aluminum replacement will be a molding with nails set in its back that can be driven through the panel. Willems advises his students to remember that "aluminum is very soft—use a swage tool to set the nails and shape the strip."

KEEPING IT SHARP

What sort of maintenance procedures does Jim Willems recommend to keep a car's interior sealed from the elements? "Treat weather strips and all vinyl with a product such as Armorall," he said. "The reason for treating a door or windshield strip, especially the door strips, which have a kind of sponge interior with a molded skin over it, is that if that skin cracks it will allow the strip to absorb lots of water and it will disentegrate as it freezes and dries out. If the strips are treated occasionally with a preservative it will seal the cracks and keep water from entering into the weatherstrip."

A rarely-used car should be treated once a year, Willems said, suggesting the pre-spring tour clean-up as a good time to perform the treatment. Cars that are left outside should be gone over every two months for sure protection. When cleaning interiors, especially vinyls or leathers, Willems said that many car owners try to clean and treat the material at the same time. "Don't treat dirty material before cleaning it and drying it," Willems said.

THE BASIC RULE

What is the one rule that Jim Willems stresses most to his students at McPherson College's auto restoration school? "How you lay out; you need to start from the center and work on out. Always center your work, measure from the center. That's extremely important. Never start at one end."

Glossary

artificial leather—vinyl or other synthetic coated fabric giving appearance of genuine leather. Often found on side and door panels in older cars, on some closed car roof coverings and in many later cars.

baste tacking—same as "stay tacking"; holding the material with partially driven tacks, allowing adjustments before they are driven home.

bias—a line diagonal to the grain or weave of a fabric. "Cutting on a bias" is cutting diagonally across a piece of material.

blind-stitch—by machine, blind-stitching is a special method used to keep the stitches invisible on one side of the fabric. Used on headliners. By hand, a blind-stitch is made with a curved needle, pushed through and drawn back through the fabric when access is inadequate to use a straight needle.

blind-tacking—a simple method for hiding tacks. The covering is reversed and tacked to a cardboard strip (usually about ½-inch wide). Then covering is folded over and stretched, hiding the cardboard and tacks.

burlap—the coarse woven cloth made of jute used to cover springs and base fabrics. Easy to work and tear-resistant.

carpet binding—binding, usually with single lap seams on each side, cut on the bias so it can be notched for rounding corners.

coconut fiber—curled, short fibers obtained from coconuts, used as upholstery filling.

cotton felt—cotton as it is prepared for use as cushion padding.

covered buttons—buttons covered with material used for decoration. Standard-size buttons are covered by a press and die.

crushed grain leather—leather which has been processed to accent the natural grain; may also apply to artificially grained leather.

curled hair—hair from various animals twisted into ropes to give curl, then cut and used as stuffing, especially in early cars.

curved needle—special sewing needle curved into a half circle to stitch where acess is limited to opposite side. Leather sewing requires triangular cross section curved hand needle.

denim—material from which jeans are made; strong, inexpensive, it is used to cover padding and keep it in place. Last layer before final cover.

escutcheon—metal trim plates or grommets in automobiles.

filling—the stuffing in pleats, diamonds, etc.; a variety of fillers are used, including down, hair coconut fiber, sisal, kapok and cotton.

flat fabric—cloth without pile or other raised surface, common examples are broadcloth, bedford cord, whipcord.

flys—pieces of more economical material used to extend a covering into hidden areas of a cushion.

framing lace—similar to windlace, with a tube core, but smaller and usually used to cover seams or places where trim portions join.

fullness—extra space, figured into pattern, allowing for filling pleats and tufts. One inch of fullness allows the material to raise one inch above the surface when filling is added.

hair—once the favorite filling of auto builders. Horse manes and tails made the best hair, still obtainable but other fillings are usually substituted.

hammer (upholsterer's)—the main tool of the trimming trade, a light-weight hammer, slightly curved head, double-faced. One face is magnetized to hold tacks while positioning. Other side is used to drive home tacks.

hidem binding—binding, usually of imitation leather, with two folds formed over wires. Binding is opened up, tacks are driven in exposed center channel, then are covered by pressing the sections together which are held in place by the wires.

leather—tanned animal hides, usually taken from cattle. Many grades available. Vat-dyed leather has color all through it; other leather has color sprayed or painted on surface only.

mohair—fleece of Angora goats, woven into cotton or wool and treated with a rubberized backing; mohair was long a favorite interior material for automakers.

morocco leather—the tanned hide of goats.

muslin—cotton fabric, open weave, used for covering inner components in cushions.

pile fabric—upholstery covering, such as mohair, with a nap woven into a backing. Nap consists of upright strands. Durable and attractive, velours and velvets are also pile fabrics.

pleats—folds, usually with a hidden seam, appearing at regular intervals in covering upholstery. Pleats use filler to build up fullness.

Randall molding—upholstery cloth or lace wrapped around half-round rubber or rattan core, with metal nailing strip on the inner face. Used in older cars to finish seat backs and for decoration.

regulator—handy upholsterer's tool, flat one end, pointed on the other, about 8-inches long. Used to distribute lumps in filling, for popping woven fabric over brad heads and many other tasks.

robe cord—upholstered cord, usually attached to the seat back panel in sedans. Originally used to hold lap robes in the days before heaters.

selvedge—an edge of a woven fabric finished to prevent raveling.

spring removing tool—special tool for removing clip springs on door and window regulators, especially on GM cars.

stay tacking—baste tacking; holding the material with partially driven tacks.

top grain leather—the horizontal section of a hide with the original outer surface grain intact.

warp—lengthwise threads in woven fabrics. Filler is woven around the warp to give a finish on flat fabrics.

windlace or windcord—fabric or leather wrapped around solid or hollow rubber tubing, leaving a skirt for tacking or otherwise attaching. Used along edges of center body pillar, around door openings, etc., to keep out wind and water.

wire-on molding—binding, usually of imitation leather, has a skirt for tacking, molding strip has wire which holds it in place when folded over tacking strip. Usually has half-round cross-section.

Appendix

CAR CLUB DIRECTORY

Joining a club devoted to the preservation of the make of car you own, plus obtaining a membership in one of the national multi-make organizations embracing the era in which your car was built, can aid your interior restoration in many ways. This club directory contains address information current at the time of publication. Some clubs may change addresses as time passes.

NATIONAL MULTI-MAKE ORGANIZATIONS
Antique Cars

Antique Automobile Club of America, Inc. 501 West Governor Rd., Hershey, Pa. 17033.

Horseless Carriage Club of America. 9031 E. Florence Ave., Arrington Square, Downey, Calif. 90240.

Mid-America Old Time Auto Association. 1799 Mignon, Memphis, Tenn. 38107.

Steam Automobile Club of America. 333 N. Michigan Ave., Chicago, Ill. 60601.

Veteran Motor Car Club of America. Office of the Executive Secretary, Dr. Robert H. DeHart, 105 Elm St., Andover, Mass. 01810.

Classic Cars (1925-1948 Selected Makes)

Classic Car Club of America. P.O. Box 443, Madison, N.Y. 07940.

"Action Era" Cars (1928-1950)

Contemporary Historical Vehicle Association. 1124 W. Fern Dr., Fullerton, CA 92633.

Postwar Cars (1945-1964)

The Milestone Car Society. 7665 East 75th St., Indianapolis, Ind. 46256.

Sports Cars

Vintage Sports Car Club of America, Inc. 170 Wetherhill Rd., Garden City, N.Y. 11530.

Vintage Sports Car Drivers Assoc. 125 W. Hubbard St., Chicago, Ill. 60611.

Commercial And Specialty Vehicles

American Truck Historical Society. Saunders Building, 201 Office Park Drive, Birmingham, Ala. 35223.

Antique Truck Club of America. 8-9 115th St., College Point, N.Y. 11356.

Society for the Preservation & Appreciation of Antique Motor Fire Apparatus. P.O. Box 450 Eastwood Station, Syracuse, N.Y. 13206.

Military Vehicle Collectors' Club. P.O. Box 503, Broomfield, Colo. 80020.

Motor Bus Society, Inc. P.O. Box 7058, West Trenton, N.J. 08628.

National Panel Delivery Club. 4002½ Hermitage Rd., Richmond, Va. 23227.

National Street Rod Assoc. 3041 Getwell, #301, Memphis, Tenn. 38118.

National Woodie Club. 5522 W. 140th St., Hawthorne, Calif. 90250.

INDIVIDUAL OR CORPORATE MARQUE CLUBS

AC

The AC Owners Club. American Centre, 44 Barrett St., Needham, Mass. 02192.

Ahrens-Fox

Ahren-Fox Fire Buffs Association. Box 233, Rte. 2, Schwenksville, Pa. 19473.

Alfa-Romeo

Alfa-Romeo Owners Club. Box 331, Northbrook, Ill. 60062.

Allard

Allard Owners Club USA. 33 Lenderwood Rd., Montville, N.J. 07045.

American Austin

American Austin-Bantam Club. Box 328, Morris, N.Y. 13803.

Amilcar

The Amilcar Register. c/o D.W. Peacock, Esq., 27 Farnborough Crescent, Addington, Surrey, England.

AMX

Classic AMX Club International. 5731 Walker Ave., Loves Park, Ill. 61111.

Classic AMX Club. 1135 Bloomwood Rd., San Pedro, Calif., 90732.

Armstrong-Siddeley

Armstrong-Siddeley Owners Club Ltd. 90 Alumhurst Rd., Westbourne, Bournemouth, Hampshire, England.

Arnolt-Bristol

Arnolt-Bristol Registry. 9832 Gina Drive, West Chester, Ohio 45069.

Aston Martin

Aston Martin Owners Club. WSA Centre, 195 Mount Paran Rd. NW, Atlanta, Ga. 30327.

Auburn

Auburn-Cord-Duesenberg Club Inc. P.O. Box 100, Skippack, Pa., 19474.

Austin

Vintage Austin Register. 17 Grove Park Ave., Sittingbourne, Kent, England.

Austin-Healey

Austin-Healey Sports & Touring Club. P.O. Box 3539, York, Pa. 17402.

Avanti

Avanti Owners Assoc. International. 1470 Sylvan Ave., Trumbull, Conn. 06611

Bentley

Bentley Drivers Club, Ltd. 76A High St., Long Crendon, Bucks, England.

BMW

BMW Car Club of America. Box 96, Boston, Mass. 02199.

BMW Automobile Club of America. P.O. Box 401, Hollywood, Calif. 90028.

Bugatti

American Bugatti Club. 8724 E. Garvey Ave., Rosemead, Calif. 91770.

Buick

Buick Club of America. P.O. Box 898, Garden Grove, Calif. 92642.

McLaughlin-Buick Club of Canada. 99 Simcoe St., Oshawa, Ontario, Canada.

Cadillac

Cadillac-LaSalle Club. 3340 Poplar Dr., Warren, Mich., 48091.

Chevrolet

Early Four-Cylinder Chevrolet Club International. 11948 Highdale St., Norwalk, Calif. 90650.

National Nomad Club. P.O. Box 606, Arvada, Colo. 80002.

Tri-Chevy Assoc. 433 W. 15th St., Chicago Heights, Ill. 60411.

Vagabonds of America. 7905 Greenleaf Ave., Whittier, Calif., 90602.

Vintage Chevrolet Club of America. P.O. Box 5387, Orange, Calif. 92667.

Chrysler

Airflow Club of America, Inc. RD 1, Arkport, N.Y. 14807.

Chrysler 300 Club. 629 Berkley Ave., Elmhurst, Ill. 60126.

Chrysler 300 Club International Inc. 19 Donegal Ct., Ann Arbor, Mich. 48104.

National Chrysler Products Club, Inc. P.O. Box 326, Vincentown, N.H. 08088.

The Imperial Owners Club. P.O. Box 991, Scranton, Pa. 18503.

Walter P. Chrysler Club. Box 4705, No. Hollywood, Calif. 91607.

Continental (Non-Lincoln)

Continental Registry. 240 Greenridge N.W., Grand Rapids, Mich. 49594.

Corvair

Corvair Society of America. P.O. Box 2488, Pensacola, Fla. 32503.

Corvette

National Corvette Owners Association. 404 S. Maple Ave, Falls Church, Va. 22046.

National Corvette Restorers Society. 63370 CR 19, Rt. 5, Goshen, Ind. 46526.

Vintage Corvette Club of America. Box T, Atascadero, Calif. 93422.

Crosley

Crosley Automobile Club, Inc. 4825 Ridge Rd., East, Williamson, N.Y. 14289.

Daimler

The Daimler & Lanchester Owners Club. c/o H.D. Saunders, Esq., Eastgate House, Appleby Magna, Burton-on-Trent, England.

Delage

Les Amis De Delage. Siege Social et Secretariat, Chateau des Ducs de Bretagne, 44-Nantes, France.

Delahaye

Delahaye Club. c/o Jean-Pierre Bernard, Les Milans, La Celle, St. Cloud, France.

DeSoto

DeSoto Club of America. 105 E. 96, Kansas City, Mo. 64114.

Dodge

Club Dodge. P.O. Box 12150C, Scranton, Pa. 18501.
Daytona-Superbird Auto Club. 13717 W. Green Meadow Dr., New Berlin, Wis. 53151.
Daytona-Superbird Assoc. 507 Monticello Blvd., Alexandria, Va. 22305.

Durant

Durant Family Registry. 2700 Timberlane, Green Bay, Wis. 54303.

Edsel

Edsel Owners Club. P.O. Box 764, Alamo, Calif. 94507.
Edsel Owners Club Inc. West Liberty, Ill. 62425.
The International Edsel Club. P.O. Box 69, Belvidere, In 61008.

Erskine

Erskine Register. 441 East Saint Clair, Almont, Mich. 48003.

Facel Vega

Facel Vega Club. Box 295, Novi, Mich. 48050.

Ferrari

Ferrari Club of America. 6250 Woodward Ave., Detroit, Mich. 48202.

Fiat

Fiat Club of America. Box 192, Sommerville, Mass. 02143.

Ford

Early Ford V-8 Club of America. P.O. Box 2122, San Leandro, Calif. 94577.

Early Ford Rachero Registry. P.O. Box 1796, Sequim, Wash. 98382.

Fabulous Fifties Ford Club. Box 33263, Granada Hills, Calif. 91344.

Ford Mercury Club of America. P.O. Box 3551, Hayward, Calif. 94540.

International Ford Retractable Club, Inc. RFD 5, Bryan, Ohio 43506.

Model A Ford Club of America, Inc. P.O. Box 1791, Whittier, Calif. 90603.

Model A Restorers Club, Inc. P.O. Box 1930A, Dearborn, Mich. 48121.

Model T Ford Club of America. Box 7400, Burbank, Calif., 91510.

The Model T Ford Club International. P.O. Box 915, Elgin, Ill. 60120.

The Mustang Club of America, Inc. P.O. Box 447, Lithonia, Ga. 30058.

Mustang Owners Club. 2829 Cagua Dr. N.E., Albuquerque, N.M. 87110.

Retractable Ford Club. 201 Hillcrest Dr., Carlinville, Ill. 62626.

Shelby American Automobile Club. 415 Dorchester Ave., Lincoln Park, Reading, Pa. 19609.

Franklin

H.H. Franklin Club, Cazenovia College, Cazenovia, N.Y. 13035.

Frazer-Nash

Frazer-Nash Section, Vintage Sports Car Club. 65 Coventry St., Didderminster, Worcs., DY10 2Bs, England.

Graham and Graham-Paige

Graham Owners Club International. P.O. Box 105, Burlington, Mass. 01803.

Haynes

Haynes and Apperson Owners Club. 409 E. Walnut St., Kokomo, Ind. 46901.

Hispano-Suiza

Hispano-Suiza Society. 230 Park Ave., Suite 1624, New York, N.Y. 10017.

Hudson

Hudson-Essex-Terraplane, Inc. 100 E. Gross, Ypsilanti, Mich. 48197.

Hupmobile

Hupmobile Club, Inc. 5457 Tannerwood Dr., Reno, NV 89511.

International

International Truck Restorers Assoc. 2026 Bayer Ave. Fort Wayne, Ind. 46805.

Isotta-Fraschini

Isotta-Fraschini Owners Association. 9704 Illinois St., Hebron, Ill. 60034.

Jaguar

Jaguar Clubs of America. 600 Willow Tree Road, Leonia, N.J. 07605.

Jeepster

Willys Overland Jeepster Club, Inc. Box 12042, El Paso, Texas 79912.
Midstates Jeepster Assoc. 4038 S. Grove Ave., Stickney, Ill. 60402.

Jowett

Jowett Car Club. c/o A. Pluckrose, Esq., "The Briars," Castledon Rd., Downham, Billericay, CM11 L1H, England.

Kaiser

Kaiser Frazer Owners Club International. 4130 New River Stage, New River, Arizona, 85029.

Kissel

Kissel Kar Klub. c/o E.E. Husting,, Frost Pond Rd., Locust Valley, N.Y. 11560.

Lafayette

Lafayette Owners Club of America. 176½ East 75th St., New York, N.Y. 10021.

Lagonda

The Lagonda Club. c/o Robert Crane, 10 Crestwood Trail, Sparta, N.J. 07871.

Lancia

American Lancia Club. 50 Mansion Rd., Springfield, Pa. 19064.

Lincoln

Lincoln Zephyr Owners Club. P.O. Box 185, Middletown, Pa. 17057.

Lincoln Continental Owners Club. P.O. Box 549, Nogales, Arizona 85621.

Continental Mark II Owners Association. 3621 West Burbank Blvd., Burbank, Calif. 91505.

Lotus

Club Elite. Box 351, Clarksville, Tenn. 37040.

Lotus West. Box 75972, Los Angeles, Calif. 90005.

Marmon

Marmon Register. 5364 Stuart Ave., S.E., Grand Rapids, Mich. 49508.

Mercedes-Benz

Gull Wing Group. Box 2093, Sunnyvale, Calif. 94087.

Mercedes-Benz Club of America. Box 4550, Chicago, Ill. 60680.

Mercer

Mercer Associates. c/o Prof. Cain, Dept. of Business Administration, Texas Tech, Lubbock, Texas 79409.

Messerschmitt

Heinkel-Messerschmitt-Isetta Club. 1224 Highland Ave., Union, N.J. 07083.

Messerschmitt Owners Club, USA. 39 Sylvan Way, West Caldwell, N.J. 07006.

Metz

Metz Register. c/o Franklin B. Tucker, 216 Central Ave., West Caldwell, N.J. 07006.

MG

MG Car Club Ltd. 600 Willow Tree Road, Leonia, N.J. 07605.

American MGB Assoc. 111 Roger Ave., Inwood, N.Y. 11696.

North American MG Register. 5 Miller Fall Ct., Derwood, Md. 20855.

Classic MG Club. 1307 Ridgecrest Rd., Orlando, Fla. 32806.

Morgan

Morgan Three-Wheeler Club, U.S. Group. 8 Leewer Ct., Rye, N.Y. 10508.

Morgan Car Club of Washington, D.C., Inc. 616 Gist Ave., Silver Spring, Md. 20910.

Nash

Metropolitan Owners Club of North America. 104 Marion Ct., Jacksonville, N.C. 28540.

Nash Metropolitan Club of Calif. 2244 Cross St., LaCanada, Calif. 91011.

Metropolitan Owners Club of America. 49 Carleton St., Westbury, N.Y. 11590.

The Nash Car Club of America. 10703 Allendale, Woodstock, Ill. 60098.

Nash-Healey

Nash-Healey Car Club, Int. 100 Church St., Lakeland, Ga. 31635.

NSU

NSU Enthusiasts USA. RD #2, Corning, N.Y. 14830.

Oldsmobile

The Oldsmobile Club of America, Inc. Jerry Walker, P.O. Box 21696, St. Louis, Mo. 63109.

Oldsmobile Club of America. 145 Latona Rd., Rochester, N.Y. 14626.

Curved-Dash Olds Club. 3455 Florida Ave. No., Minneapolis, Minn. 55427.

Packard

Packards International Motor Car Club. 302 French St., Santa Ana, Calif. 92701.

The Packard Club (Packard Automobile Classics Inc.) P.O. Box 2808, Oakland, Calif. 94618.

Pierce-Arrow

Pierce-Arrow Society, Inc. 135 Edgerton St., Rochester, N.Y. 14607.

Plymouth

Plymouth 4&6 Cylinder Owners Club, Inc. 203 Main St. East, Cavalier, N.D. 58220.

Pontiac (& Oakland)

Classic G.T.O. Club of Wisconsin. 840 Stroller Ave., Algoma, Wis. 54201

Pontiac-Oakland Club International, Inc. P.O. Box 5108, Salem, Ore. 97304.

Trans Am Club. P.O. Box 917, Champaign, Ill. 61820.

Porsche

Porsche Club of America. Dept IR, 5616 Claremont Dr., Alexandria, Va. 22310.

Railton

Railton Owners Club. B. McKenzie (Sec.), Fairmiles, Barnes Hall Rd.,Burncross, Sheffield, England.

REO

The REO Club of America. Rte. 2, Box 180, Forest, Ohio 45843.

Rickenbacker

The Rickenbacker Club. R.D. #5, Schenectady, N.Y. 12306.

Riley

The Riley Motor Club, Ltd. The Gables, Hinksey Hill, Oxford, England OXI 5BH.

Rolls-Royce

The Rolls-Royce Owners Club, Inc. RROC Administrative Office, 1822 N. 2nd St. Harrisburg, Pa. 17102.

Singer

Singer Owners Club. 31 Rivershill, Watton-at-Stone, Hertfordshire, England.

Simplex

Simplex Automobile Club. Meadow Spring, Glen Cove, N.Y. 11542.

Stevens-Duryea

Stevens-Duryea Associates. 3565 Newhaven Rd., Pasadena, Calif. 91007.

Studebaker

Antique Studebaker Club, Inc. P.O. Box 142, Monrovia, Calif. 91016.
The Studebaker Drivers Club, Inc. P.O. Box 3044, South Bend, Ind. 46619.

Thunderbird

Classic Thunderbird Club International. P.O. Box 2398, Culver City, Calif. 90230.
Vintage Thunderbird Club of America. P.O. Box 2250. Dearborn, Mich. 48123.

Triumph

Triumph Sports Owners Assoc. 600 Willow Tree Rd., Leonia, N.J. 07605.
The Vintage Triumph Register. P.O. Box 36477, Grosse Pointe, Mich. 48236.

Tucker

The Tucker Auto Club of America. P.O. Box 1027, Orange Park, Fla. 32073.

Will St. Clair

The Wills Club. 705 S. Clyde Ave., Kissimmee, Fla. 32741.

Willys

Willys Club. 509 W. Germantown Pike, Norristown, Pa. 19403.
Willys-Overland-Knight Registry, Inc. 2754 Lullington Dr., Winston-Salem, N.C. 27103.

Wolseley

The Wolseley Register. 17 Hills Ave., Cambridge, England CB1 4UY.

SUPPLIERS

The firms listed are among those currently offering supplies, materials and services to the old car hobbyist. Additional sources may be found in club and general hobbyist periodicals. Correspondence with hobby suppliers should always include a self-addressed, stamped envelope (SASE) for the response.

Carpets

Auto Mat Co. 223 Park Avenue, Hicksville, N.Y. 11802. Nylon hi-pile and deep twist carpets for most 1950-1980 cars. Also leatherette door panel materials in 54" rolls. (See Materials Suppliers for additional carpet sources.)

Headliners

Acme Auto Headlining Co. P.O. Box 847, Long Beach, Calif. 90801. Headliner kits for 1928-1979 cars.
Automotive Obsolete. 1023 E. 4th St., Santa Ana, Calif. 92701. 1926-1976 custom-tailored headliner kits.

Instruments, Knobs, Radios, etc.

Audio Sound. 0-932 Chicago Dr., Jenison, Mich. 49528. Radio repair.
Bob's Speedometers. 15255 Grand River Avenue, Detroit, Mich. 48227. Gauge repair, face restoration.
Dick Evans. 45 Prospect St., Essex Junction, Vermont 05452. Repairs and rebuilds capillary tube-type temperature gauges.
Gardner-Westcott Co. 30958½ Industrial Road, Livonia, Mich. 48150. Chrome-plated nuts, bolts, fasteners.
Burnell D. Harty. Box 43, Sandy Point, Maine 04972. George W. Borg Co. clocks repaired.
W.D. Honeycutt. Box 411, LBT Hill, Hartsville, S.C. 29550. Radios repaired.

Mo-Ma Mfg. 10853 Magnolia Boulevard, North Hollywood, Calif. 91601. Gauges restored and refaced.

Nisonger Corp. 35 Bartels Place, New Rochelle, N.Y. 10801. Instrument rebuilding (British Smith and Jaeger only).

A. Petrik. 10436 Crockette, Sun Valley, Calif. 91352. Heater valves repaired.

The Radio Man. 7398 So. Leewynn, Sarasota, Fla. 33582. Radios repaired.

Reynolds Repairs. 4 Lobao Dr., Danvers, Mass. 01923. Speedometer-tachometer repairs.

Marvin Roth Antique Radios. 14500 LaBelle, Oak Park, Mich. 48237. Radios repaired.

Seckman's Antique Radio, Inc. 1048 Sunnywood Ln., Ravenna, Ohio 44266. Radios repaired.

Steve's Auto Clock Service. 7364 Alaba Ave., Yucca Valley, Calif. 92284. Auto clock repairs.

20th Century Talking Machine Co. 2530 Pleasant Hill Rd., Sebastopol, Calif. 95472. Radio repairs.

Mark Wallach, Ltd. 27 New St., Nyack-on-the-Hudson, N.Y. 10960. Interior woodwork restoration.

West Hill Auto Clocks. Wolcott, Vermont 05680. Clock repair.

Gail Westmoreland. c/o The Wickes Corp. 1010 Second Ave., San Diego, Calif. 92101. Instrument face restoration.

Paul B. Wiesman. Hydro-E-Lectric, 48-B Appleton Rd., Auburn, Mass. 01501. Power seat and window cylinders rebuilt, reproduced.

George Zahn. 493 Bay, Pontiac, Mich. 48057. Radio repairs.

Materials

Abingdon Spares Ltd., 1329 Highland Ave., Needham, Mass. 02192. Leather upholstery kits for MG's. TD & TF carpet kits.

Antique Fabric & Trim Co. Rte. 2, Box 870 C, Cambridge, Minn. 55008. Upholstery cloth, trim bindings, vinyls, fasteners.

Big "T" Parts Co. 19337 Greenview, Detroit, Mich. 48219. Carpet sets, spray vinyl colors, upholstery kits, etc.

Joel Braverman. 2149 Jones Ave., Wantagh, N.Y. 11793. Distributor for Git-Rot dry rot treatment for wood.

Classic Leather. P.O. Box 218, Centerpost, N.Y. 11721. Upholstery restoration products.

The Clausen Co. 1055 King George Rd., Fords, N.J. 08863. "Leatherique" kits for renewing leather interiors.

Stan Coleman. 320 South St., Building 12A, Morristown, N.J. 07960. Upholstery kits (incl. Model A Ford), seat cover kits, U.S. and European convertible tops, etc.

Doyle's Upholstery & Canvas Co., Inc. Box 458, Hwy. 441, Fruitland Park, Fla. 32731. Automotive trim fabrics.

Frank S. Findlay. P.O. Box 968, Manchester, Conn. 06040. "Battleship" linoleum for floorboards, etc.

Hides, Inc. Box 361, Hackettstown, N.J. 07840. Leathers, etc.

Bill Hirsch. 396 Littleton Ave., Newark, N.J. 07103. Connolly and other leathers; English and other broadcloths; Wilton, hogshair, square weave and other carpets; bindings; conv. tops, etc.

Kanter Auto Products Div., Packard Industries. 76R Monroe St., Boonton, N.J. 07008. Carpet kits, convertible tops, upholstery fabrics and kits, leathers.

King Kovers, Inc., 22357 Mission Boulevard, Hayward, Calif. 94541. Automotive trim fabrics.

Tony Lauria. R.D. 2, Box 253B, Landenberg, Penna. 19350. "Battleship" linoleum for floorboards, etc.

LeBaron Bonney Co. 14 Washington St., Amesbury, Mass. 01913. Bedford cloth, mohairs, vinyls, carpeting, bindings, fasteners, Model A & Early V-8 Ford interior kits.

Chuck Pelton. 2466 Sunset Terrace, Union Lake, Mich. 48085. Leathers.

Rae's Auto Upholstery. 186 E. Sunnyoaks Ave., Campbell, Calif. 95008. Match-up trim fabrics for 1950's to the present interiors.

"Stitts." Highway 23, Churchtown, Penna., 17555. Top and upholstery fabrics, fasteners.

Western Hide-Tex. Box 2133, Encinal Station, Sunnyvale, Calif. 94087. Leathers, mohairs, broadcloths, Bedford cords, carpeting.

The Visual Image. P.O. Box 1804, Maitland, Fla. 32751. Sports car upholstery and carpet kits.

J.C. Whitney. P.O. Box 8410, Chicago, Ill. 60680. Mail order house with many interior tools, kits and other items.

Ray Wolff. P.O. Box 18651, Milwaukee, Wis. 53218. Leathers.

Reproduction Interior Kits & Trim

All-Tru Parts Co., 375 W. Girard Ave., Madison Heights, Mich. 48071. Chevrolet and Corvette interior components.

Roger Abbott. 1199 So. El Molino, Pasadena, Calif. 91106. Clutch and brake pedal seals, etc.

Antique Auto Items. 1607 Mc Cabe Rd., Spokane, Wash. 99216. Pedal pads, etc., 1915-1950 cars.

American Mustang. 2964 Arf Ave., Hayward, Calif. 94545. 1965-67 Mustang upholstery kits, tops, etc.

California Auto Trim. 14737 Calvert St., Van Nuys, Calif. 91401. 1965-66 Mustang interior kits.

California Mustang Parts. 1249 E. Holt, Pomona, CA 91767. Manufacturer and retailer of reproduction Mustang upholstery kits, many other items.

Can Am Restoration Supply. 1203 Chicago Rd., Troy Mich. 48084. 1955-64 Chevrolet seat and trim kits, carpets, headliners, etc.

Dennis Carpenter Ford Reproductions. P.O. Box 26398, Charlotte, N.C. 28213. Trunk mats, plastic knobs, radio faces, etc. for early Ford V-8s.

Pete Ciadella Enterprises. 1876 E. 3rd St., Tempe, Ariz. 85281. 1955-64 Chevrolet interior kits and fabrics; Corvette carpet seats.

Bob Drake Ford V-8 Reproductions. P.O. Box 642, Woodland Hills, Calif. 91356. 1932-1950s Ford knobs, pedals, escutcheons, door seals, etc.

Ford Parts Obsolete. 1320 W. Willow, Long Beach, Calif. 90810. General Ford repro. line.

Glazier's Mustang Barn. 531 Wambold Rd., Souderstown, Penna 18964. Mustang interior components.

Greenland Co. P.O. Box 332, Verdugo City, Calif. 91046. Aluminum sill plates, floor and rumble seat mats, Model T Ford steering wheels, etc.

John Griffith. 308 Washington Ave., Nutley, N.J. 07110. Window shades made.

Hampton Coach Vintage Chevrolet. 70 High St., P.O. Box 665, Hampton, N.H. 03842. Chevrolet interior kits.

Bob Kirby. Box 665, San Ynez, Calif. 93460. Wood and plastic steering wheels restored.

Larry's Mustang Parts. 511 So. Raymond, Fullerton, Calif. 92631. 1965-1968 (some to 1973) Mustang interior kits, tops, etc.

Larry's Thunderbird Parts. 511 So. Raymond, Fullerton, Calif. 92631. 1955-57 T-bird interior kits and parts.

McDonald Ford Parts Co., R.R. 3, Box 61, Rockport, Ind. 47635. T-Bird and Mustang vinyl-rubber dash pads, etc.

Metro-Moulded Parts. 3031 2nd St. N. Minneapolis, Minn. 55411. Rubber parts, window channels, grommets, pads, etc.

Mustang Mart. 665 Mc Glincey Ln., Campbell, Calif. 95008. 1965-66 Mustang upholstery, carpets, door panels, etc.

Noland Tool and Chemical Co. P.O. Box 118, Alvarado, Texas 76009. Extruded door and trunk rubber strips, etc.

The Paddock. 38 W. Warrick St., Knightstown, Ind. 46418. 1965-66 Mustang interior kits and parts.

Prestige Thunderbird. 10215 Greenwood Ave., Santa Fe Springs, Calif. 90670. T-bird upholstery kits, etc.

Restoration Specialties & Supply Inc. P.O. Box 328, R.D. #2, Windber, Penna. 15963.

Lynn Steele. Rte. 1, Box 71 W, Denver, N.C. 28037. Thousands of reproduction weatherstrips, seals, grommets, etc. for all cars except 1925-1960 Fords.

Specialized Auto Parts. 301-C Adams St., Houston, Texas 77011. Ford wood, other items.

Standard Automotive. 2204 Ohio, Quincy, Ill. 62301. Model A Ford reproductions, including rumble seat mats.

Steering Wheel Service. 906 Buena Rosa Ct., Fall Brook, Calif. 92028. Plastic steering wheel rebuilding.

J. Taylor. 1251 Peggy Ave., Campbell, Calif. 95008. Reproduction 1965-66 Mustang interior kits.

TL Auto Interiors. 22721 15 Mile Rd., Mt. Clemens, Mich. 48043. 1963-64 original factory N.O.S. Ford seat covers.

Wefco Rubber Mfg. Co. 1655 Euclid Ave., Santa Monica, Calif. 90404. Rubber trim, etc.

Tops & Bows

Electron Tops. 135-11 Hillside Ave., Richmond Hill, N.Y. 11418. U.S. and European top kits.

Masonville Garage. Box 57, Masonville, Iowa 50654. Model A Ford top insert kits, rumble seat cushions.

Oak Bows. 122 Ramsey Ave., Chambersburg, Penna. 17201. Duplicates and restores wood top bows and their sockets.

Woodgraining

Dick Hedderick. Fairview Lake Rd., Tafton, Penna. 18464.

Elmo's Grainmobile. Rte. 4, Box 262, Rusk, Texas 75785.

Bill Gratkowski. 515 No. Petroleum St., Titusville, Penna. 16354.

John McNally. 209 Walnut, Jenkintown, Penna. 19046. Supplier for Di-Noc vinyl film.

Sewing Machines

Sewing Machine Distributors. 5343 Dorr St., Toledo, Ohio 43615.

Shaw's Singer Depot. 109 Drake Ave., Modesto, Calif. 95350.

Publications & Book Dealers

Auto Trim News. (For professional trimmers), 1623 Grand Ave. Baldwin, N.Y. 11510.

Car Exchange. 700 E. State St., Iola, Wis. 54945 (monthly).

Cars & Parts. P.O. Box 380, Bennington, Vermont 05201 (monthly).

Hemming Motor News. P.O. Box 380, Bennington, Vermont 05201 (monthly).

Old Cars Newspaper. 700 E. State St., Iola, Wis. 54945 (weekly).

Skinned Knuckles. (restoration journal), 175 May, Monrovia, Calif. 91016 (monthly).

Classic Motorbooks. P.O. Box 1, Osceola, Wis. 54020 (mail order auto books).

Bookman Dan. P.O. Box 13492, Baltimore, Md. 21203 (mail order auto books).

(Note: Many professional trimmers work on collector car interiors as a part of their regular trimming business. Check your area Yellow Pages. The foregoing list is far from all-inclusive.)

SCHOOLS

McPherson College. McPherson, KS 67460 (2 year automotive restoration course, includes upholstery).

RESEARCH SERVICES

Harrah's Automobile Collection. P.O. Box 10, Reno, Nevada 89431. Research service from giant library, fee charged.

RESTORATION SHOPS

Auto Exotica. 1369 Shoop Ave., Wauseon, Ohio 43567. Complete restoration, including interiors.

Automotive Restoration Inc. 50 Embree St., Stratford, Conn. 06497. General restoration, including interiors.

Chuck Bronson. Box 112, Titonka, Iowa 50480. Model A Ford restoration.

Classic Auto Restoration. 22456 Orchard Lake Rd., Farmington, Mich. 48024. General restoration, including interiors.

Classic Restoration Inc. 311-B W. 10th, Stillwater, Okla. 74074. General restoration.

Coachwork Unlimited. 370-D Commack Rd., Deer Park, N.Y. 11729. General restoration, upholstery and woodgraining.

Diamond Trim Shop. 84 Dolson Ave., Middletown, N.Y. Interiors, tops, etc.

Gaslight Automotive. 1001 Republic Dr., Unit 13, Addison, Ill. 60101. General restoration, including upholstery.

Hibernia Auto Restorations, Inc. Maple Terrace, Hibernia, N.J. 07842. Classic interior restoration and woodgraining.

J.D. Home. 314 Wilda Ln., Bozeman, Mont. 59715. Model A Ford and kit car specialist.

Interior Restorations, Etc. 3480 E. Fulton St., Columbus, Ohio 43227. Interior restoration.

Keilen's Auto Restoring. 2835 Stone St., Walpole, Mass. 02081. General restoration.

Mountain View Auto Restoration. Rte. 1, Box 71, Jewell Ridge, Va. 24622. General restoration all makes, Corvettes.

Sturm Upholstery. William Sturm, 2208 N. U.S Highway 41, Neenah, Wis. 54956. Full interior restoration, Model A Ford specialist.

Vintage Woodworks. Box 49 Iola, Wis. 54945. Cars rewooded, woodgraining, complete interior restoration.

White Post Restoration. White Post, Va. 22663. General restoration.

Index